MW01101889

Making Government Great Again

Also available from ASQ Quality Press:

A Practical Field Guide for ISO 9001:2008
Erik Valdemar Myhrberg

ISO 9001:2008 Explained, Third Edition
Charles A. Cianfrani, John E. (Jack) West, and Joseph J. Tsiakals

ISO Lesson Guide 2008: Pocket Guide to ISO 9001–2008, Third Edition
J.P. Russell and Dennis R. Arter

ISO 9001:2008 Internal Audits Made Easy: Tools, Techniques, and Step-by-Step Guidelines for Successful Internal Audits, Second Edition
Ann W. Phillips

Cracking the Case of ISO 9001:2008 for Manufacturing: A Simple Guide to Implementing Quality Management in Manufacturing, Second Edition
John E. (Jack) West and Charles A. Cianfrani

Cracking the Case of ISO 9001:2008 for Service: A Simple Guide to Implementing Quality Management in Service Organizations, Second Edition
John E. (Jack) West and Charles A. Cianfrani

Process-Driven Comprehensive Auditing: A New Way to Conduct ISO 9001:2008 Internal Audits, Second Edition
Paul C. Palmes

ISO 9001:2008 Interpretive Guide for the Design and Construction Project Team (e-Book)
Prepared by members of the ASQ Design and Construction Division and edited by John R. Broomfield

How to Audit the Process-Based QMS
Dennis R. Arter, John E. (Jack) West, and Charles A. Cianfrani

The ASQ Auditing Handbook, Third Edition
J.P. Russell, editing director

Quality Audits for Improved Performance, Third Edition
Dennis R. Arter

The Quality Toolbox, Second Edition
Nancy R. Tague

Mapping Work Processes, Second Edition
Bjørn Andersen, Tom Fagerhaug, Bjørnar Henriksen, and Lars E. Onsøyen

Root Cause Analysis: Simplified Tools and Techniques, Second Edition
Bjørn Andersen and Tom Fagerhaug

To request a complimentary catalog of ASQ Quality Press publications, call 800-248-1946, or visit our Web site at http://www.asq.org/quality-press.

Making Government Great Again

Mapping the Road to Success with ISO 9001:2008

John Baranzelli

ASQ Quality Press
Milwaukee, Wisconsin

American Society for Quality, Quality Press, Milwaukee 53203
© 2010 by ASQ
All rights reserved. Published 2009
Printed in the United States of America
15 14 13 12 11 10 09   5 4 3 2 1

Library of Congress Cataloging-in-Publication Data

Baranzelli, John.
  Making government great again : mapping the road to success with
ISO 9001:2008 / John Baranzelli.
    p. cm.
  Includes bibliographical references and index.
  ISBN 978-0-87389-779-2 (hard cover : alk. paper)
  1. Total quality management in government—United States. 2. Administrative
agencies—United States—Management. 3. Organizational change—United States.
I. Title.

  JK468.T67B37 2010
  352.3'57—dc22   2009042248

ISBN: 978-0-87389-779-2

Publisher: William A. Tony
Acquisitions Editor: Matt T. Meinholz
Project Editor: Paul O'Mara
Production Administrator: Randall Benson

ASQ Mission: The American Society for Quality advances individual, organizational,
and community excellence worldwide through learning, quality improvement, and
knowledge exchange.

Attention Bookstores, Wholesalers, Schools, and Corporations: ASQ Quality Press
books, videotapes, audiotapes, and software are available at quantity discounts with
bulk purchases for business, educational, or instructional use. For information,
please contact ASQ Quality Press at 800-248-1946, or write to ASQ Quality Press,
P.O. Box 3005, Milwaukee, WI 53201-3005.

To place orders or to request a free copy of the ASQ Quality Press Publications
Catalog, including ASQ membership information, call 800-248-1946. Visit our
Web site at www.asq.org or http://www.asq.org/quality-press.

Printed in the United States of America

 Printed on acid-free paper

Quality Press
600 N. Plankinton Avenue
Milwaukee, Wisconsin 53203
Call toll free 800-248-1946
Fax 414-272-1734
www.asq.org
http://www.asq.org/quality-press
http://standardsgroup.asq.org
E-mail: authors@asq.org

Table of Contents

List of Figures
and Tables

To the Reader

Amidst the excitement and exhilaration of quality improvement initiatives, it is important to remember that the ultimate purpose of quality management is to improve the quality of our *lives*. If quality improvements to products and services do not help us create a better world, what's the point?

The men and women of the Make-A-Wish Foundation have been in the business of improving the quality of life for nearly 30 years. Their mission is to grant wishes to children with life-threatening medical conditions to enrich the human experience with hope, strength, and joy. One hundred percent of the author's royalties for this book have been donated to the Make-A-Wish Foundation of Illinois. By purchasing this book, you have made it possible for this incredible organization to grant a wish for a child who desperately needs the gifts of hope, strength, and joy. Through the power of this wish, you have already changed the world in ways you can not possibly comprehend.

Pretty cool, huh?

If you would like to find out more information about the Make-A-Wish Foundation, I encourage you to visit their Web site at www.wish.org.

Thank you for your support,
John

Author's Note

For the sake of brevity, I have chosen to use "ISO 9001" or "the standard" when referring to the ISO 9001:2008 standard within the pages of this book. In the instances where a reference to a different ISO standard was necessary or where I referenced a specific certification (previous or current), I have referenced the applicable version to ensure adequate traceability for the reader.

Preface

"I don't care what you tell me, John," she said. "I've worked in the public sector for more than 20 years and I'm telling you that it's impossible to run a government agency like a private business because private companies have a bottom line and we don't."

It was the summer of 2004, and I was speaking with an executive of the Illinois Department of Transportation about my latest assignment. Something called ISO 9001 was supposed to revolutionize the way we conducted business, and it was my responsibility to implement it within my office (at that time it was the ISO 9001:2000 version). What is so striking about this encounter isn't the executive's retort—it is my general agreement with her statement that now strikes me as shocking. Like many of my fellow employees, I had somehow bought into the idea that a government organization is fundamentally different from a private business.

The past four years of my life has drastically changed my perspective. Coordinating and managing the implementation of an ISO 9001 management system within the context of a large public-sector organization has taught me that what I once believed was incorrect. While it's true that the financial bottom line is important to every business, I've learned that truly successful organizations also keep a watchful eye on another bottom line—the satisfaction of their customers. These organizations understand the importance of meeting the requirements of their customers and exceeding their expectations whenever possible. Cost-saving measures and effective budget control may keep a company from sinking into the depths of a stormy sea, but customer satisfaction is the wind that fills the sails and moves the ship forward.

This book is my attempt to share this journey of self-discovery with you. While written through the lens of a public-sector organization, the principles and techniques discussed in this book can be employed in any organization. It is my belief that the current push for increased social responsibility in the corporate world will result in corporations embracing some of the more progressive practices of government organizations. It's true that public-sector agencies can learn a lot from the private sector. It's also true that the private sector can benefit from successful government practices.

The pillars of this book are the eight quality management principles of the ISO 9000:2005 standard. I believe the most effective way to implement the ISO 9001 standard in any organization is to focus the effort on implementing these eight fundamentals. In this book, the major requirements of the ISO 9001 standard are explained within the context of these quality management principles.

The path to ISO 9001 certification can be a strenuous journey. I encourage you to take your time and remember that the end goal isn't certification—it's the establishment of effective policies and procedures that improve the ability of your employees to satisfy the needs of your customers and exceed their expectations. Realize that Rome wasn't built in a day and understand that if your focus becomes the achievement of certification in record time, you'll end up with a certificate to hang on your wall and little else. If you pace yourself and concentrate on meeting the standard's requirements with the goal of enhancing the ability of your employees to succeed, you'll not only become ISO 9001 certified—you'll have created a customer-focused organization that embraces a culture of continual improvement. That's truly a worthwhile achievement!

Congratulations to you for embarking on this adventure. Good luck!

Acknowledgments

T he road to success is rarely traveled alone, and this is especially true in regard to the development of this book. I'd like to take this opportunity to acknowledge the contributions of the following people.

To the men and women of the Illinois Department of Transportation: ISO 9001 certification was your achievement, not mine. The dedication and commitment to excellence you continue to demonstrate on a daily basis never ceases to amaze me.

To Vince Madonia: Thank you for providing the working title for this book. By now you have realized I used a different title for the final product. I didn't think the world was yet ready to fully appreciate the genius of your wit.

To John Webber: As ISO management representative these past five years you have been supportive, inspirational, and compassionate. I have learned to so very much from you. You have been the kind of leader that I hope to become one day.

To Christy Brown: You gave me new eyes with which to see the myriad possibilities surrounding me. Your gift is one that I will always cherish.

To Roy Baranzelli: Dad, from you I inherited the gift of determination and resolve (some unenlightened people prefer to call it stubbornness). When it came to this book, your gift was the difference between conception and completion.

To Bonnie Baranzelli: Mom, when I was a child you instilled in me a love of storytelling, and your gift can be seen throughout this book wherever an anecdote or a simple story is used to explain a complex concept. You were my first teacher and you are still my favorite.

To Angela Yoder: Sis, you have created in me a burning desire to better understand the complexities of the human mind. Your contributions can be seen wherever the concepts of psychology are discussed within the pages of this book.

To Nicholas Baranzelli: Son, you are the reason I draw breath each day. During the past five years your support, encouragement, and understanding have been remarkable to say the least. While everyone else on this list provided assistance, you provided the most important element of all: purpose. I hope I made you proud.

To Diana Sternitzke: What can I say? For the past five years you and I have been a team. No one has pushed me harder, made me laugh louder, or raised my blood pressure higher than you. You have been the yin to my yang (or is it the other way around?). The opposite of me in so many ways, you provided the catalyst for personal growth I desperately needed and the structure necessary to harness my strengths. Without you none of this would have been possible.

1
Introduction

Climb high, climb far
Your goal the sky, your aim the star.

—Inscription on Hopkins Memorial Steps,
Williams College, Williamstown, Massachusetts

Have you ever looked into a clear night sky and marveled at the incredible number of stars? Over the centuries, the stars above have evoked a sense of awe and wonder in adults and children alike. On the clearest of evenings the stars seem so numerous they look like a blanket that we could grab and wrap around our bodies as we drift off to sleep.

Do you realize that most of the stars in the evening sky can't be seen by the naked eye? Astronomers tell us that ninety-nine percent of the stars in the universe simply do not produce enough energy in order for us to see them. These stars have been named red dwarfs. Red dwarfs are stars that burned bright for a short time but did not have the proper structure necessary to keep the core hot and active. Because the cores of these stars grew cool, they contracted and can no longer be seen. The stars that you and I *can* see in the evening sky are extremely rare in the universe. These highly luminous stars are elegant creations of nature that have developed a perfect balance between the internal and external forces that define them.

Because the mass of these stars is so large, the gravity at the center is tremendous—so tremendous that it actually forces hydrogen atoms to fuse together to form a new, larger element. The fusion of these hydrogen atoms releases an astounding amount of energy—part of which we see as the visible light that reaches us here on earth. This energy release keeps the interior of the star hot and the gas pressure high. That pressure balances the force of the star's gravity and prevents it from contracting. The star reaches a perfect balance between the gravity pushing inward and the pressure and energy pushing outward. This perfect balance between competing forces is what allows a star to shine for the entire world to see.

Organizations are no different than stars. The best organizations have reached a delicate balance between the energy produced internally and the structure that holds them together. These organizations use structure to keep the core of their business hot and active and to hold the organization together. This structure causes individuals to bond together into teams and work together to produce amazing results. It focuses the entire organization on specific objectives in a way that provides total clarity for everyone involved. It is this structure that allows these organizations to shine.

We call this structure a *management system.* A management system is nothing mysterious. It is simply a set of policies and procedures that govern an organization. Most organizations have a management system of some sort. What differentiates one management system from another are the types of controls and requirements that comprise its structure. Organizations with weak management systems can't focus the energy that is generated from improvement initiatives, and as a consequence the activity stops, the core cools, and the organization fades into a background of mediocrity.

Does any of this sound familiar?:

- We've tried various improvement techniques in the past but they seem to die out after a few months.

- We develop some great ideas but no one ever seems to follow up on them.

- Many of our initiatives seem to lose momentum and disappear.

- The last improvement initiative we tried created a lot of extra work for everyone and didn't really help us out very much in the long run.

In an attempt to ignite a reaction in the core of an organization, management often reaches for the latest and greatest strategic planning or quality improvement technique. When these initiatives are introduced, there is typically a lot of activity and meetings in the beginning that generate genuine enthusiasm and intense effort. Unfortunately, the newness usually wears off quickly, and "business as usual" becomes the norm once again. The employees who embraced the endeavor and worked hard to make it a success quickly become disillusioned and disenchanted. They feel as if all the hard work they expended on this effort has been wasted because nothing has really changed within the organization. Paradoxically, the effort to improve motivation and employee engagement often causes morale to plunge. How can we avoid this potential pitfall of most improvement initiatives?

A properly designed and effectively implemented management system can prevent the collapse of important improvement initiatives while maintaining the pressure needed to keep the core of the organization hot and active. Standards like ISO 9001 can help take the guesswork out of the construction of an effective management system. These standards contain decades of best practices combined with the latest research in the areas of quality improvement and organizational management.

IDOT'S EXPERIENCE

In 2003, management at the Illinois Department of Transportation (IDOT) faced a bleeding budget and a bleak future. The agency had just suffered a massive loss of staff through a statewide early retirement initiative when the governor's office and the Illinois legislature began work to fill a $2 billion dollar gap in the annual budget caused by unfunded pension liabilities. The economic dilemma that the state was facing meant that most of the positions vacated by the early retirement initiative would not be filled. IDOT was home to some of the most talented employees in the state, but cracks had begun to form in the structure of the organization due to the loss of staff. Changes needed to be made. Processes that had worked well when the agency had a head count of more than 7000 employees needed to be revised to account for the new head count number, which had fallen below 6000 for the first time in the history of the organization. IDOT was facing some serious challenges to its core mission capability because of the staggering loss of institutional knowledge, a reduced operating budget, and an increasing demand for public accountability. The agency needed a fresh approach.

In early 2004, secretary of transportation Tim Martin met with key staff members to discuss the challenges facing IDOT. The secretary was very interested in the progress of IDOT's Strategic Planning Initiative. The assistant to the secretary for policy, strategies, and organization, John Webber, explained to the secretary that IDOT was having difficulty addressing some key strategic issues. John believed that improvements in areas like training, management effectiveness, and communication could increase employee productivity but explained that IDOT had been unable to make measurable improvements in these key areas. Excellent targets and goals had been developed but little or no progress had been made.

Multiple improvement initiatives had been introduced—many began quite promisingly—but all had fallen short of creating sustainable change. These teams had been led by some of the brightest leaders in the entire organization. Most of these teams had quickly fused together, and a great amount of energy and enthusiasm was created. Unfortunately, the lack of structure within the organization caused the initial energy to dissipate rapidly. Many employees involved in these improvement initiatives quickly grew disenchanted and embittered as they saw little improvement resulting from all of their hard work. These improvement initiatives were undertaken to improve employee attitudes. Ironically, morale plummeted in IDOT employee surveys as these initiatives failed to realize their goals.

The organization lacked focus. The organization lacked *structure.*

Secretary Martin believed IDOT needed the focus and framework that a management system could provide. Secretary Martin instructed John Webber to investigate the ISO 9001 standard to determine if it could be a good fit for the agency. John researched the ISO 9001 standard and discussed its feasibility with IDOT management for several weeks. He concluded that such an endeavor would be difficult to complete in a public organization like IDOT, but if successful would greatly benefit the agency and help address some key strategic concerns.

The agency selected SAIC (Science Applications International Corporation), of McLean, Virginia, to assist in the training and registration effort by providing consulting services. Dr. Walter R. McCollum helped IDOT employees understand proper ways to apply the ISO 9001 standard in a transportation agency. Over the course of 15 months, key processes were identified, reviewed, and revised as needed, a document control system was created, and an internal quality system audit program was developed. Later in the process, QAI, Inc. and Lloyd's Register Quality Assurance were selected to provide additional training that helped the agency further develop and improve the quality management system.

I won't lie to you—the first few months were confusing, and it often seemed like we were taking two steps back for every three steps forward. Our document control strategy changed several times, our internal audit program had to be completely redesigned, and nobody could seem to figure out how to measure the effectiveness of their processes. We made many mistakes but we gained a wealth of understanding from each one. We tripped, stumbled, and fell down flat on our face more than once, but each time we made significant progress. For the first time in many years, we were creating sustainable change—and man, was that fun!

Our management system was in its infancy, and like all new parents we dealt with the occasional temper tantrums and sleepless nights. But as this system began to mature, our organization improved. The structure provided by this new management system kept improvement initiatives moving forward by enforcing deadlines, providing accountability, and keeping IDOT top management focused and committed. This structure kept improvement teams actively engaged and allowed the energy and enthusiasm to build until the old organization began to shine once again.

In the summer of 2005, NSF-ISR, an NSF International company, thoroughly assessed the IDOT quality management system and found it to be in compliance with ISO 9001:2000 standard requirements. On June 18, 2005, IDOT achieved ISO 9001:2000 registration for 23 key processes primarily located in the central administrative office and regional district six. On July 6, 2006, that registration was successfully expanded to encompass all processes involved in the planning, design, and construction of road and bridge improvements, maintenance of existing roads and bridges, and administrative oversight in the central administrative office and district six—both headquartered in Springfield, Illinois. We became the first state transportation agency in the country to achieve ISO 9001:2000 certification for its major business processes. In July of 2009, we successfully transitioned to the newest version of the standard—ISO 9001:2008.

SUMMARY

Many organizations struggle with the proper execution of strategy. The problem generally isn't the strategy that has been developed, nor is it the employees who have been empowered to implement it. In my experience, the issue is generally a lack of sufficient structure necessary to keep improvement initiatives moving forward. A management system based on the requirements of the ISO 9001 standard can improve the ability of organizations to implement their strategy and achieve their goals.

If your organization has been unable to create sustainable change, if initiatives in your organization quickly lose momentum and disappear, if previous organizational improvement techniques have been attempted with little or no success, you should consider the development of a management system for your organization. In my opinion, there is no better model for an effective management system than the ISO 9001 standard.

If you are interested in learning how to harness the power of ISO 9001 in your organization, if you want to create sustainable change, if you want to be one of those rare, bright stars that the world gazes at with awe— read on!

2

Quality Management Systems

Listen to me, and in five years you will be competing with the West. Keep listening, and soon the West will be demanding protection from you.

—W. Edwards Deming,
speaking to Japanese industrialists circa 1950

In the late 1970s, Japanese manufacturers began to grab market share from American companies at an alarming rate. The quality of Japanese products far exceeded that of their American competitors, and consumers began to abandon American products in droves. American executives grew fearful of their Japanese counterparts as the trade deficit of the United States began to grow at a frightening pace. Many American executives asked themselves, how could this have happened? In the 1950s and 1960s, American manufacturing ruled the world. In less than three decades, a small country decimated by war and extremely poor in natural resources went from producing products that were cheap and barely worth the price to an economic powerhouse that was now threatening the economic stability of the mighty United States of America! American executives scrambled to learn Japan's methods.

What they found amazed them. Japanese manufacturers were achieving incredible levels of efficiency in their production processes. Their employees were highly engaged, well trained, and committed to quality and customer satisfaction. The Japanese were using quality objectives with gusto to drive continual improvement of the organization. These objectives were translated into action using exceptionally innovative methods such as kanban (just in time) and quality control circles. Production waste was minimal and the level of quality was astounding. Where American manufacturers were producing parts with tolerances of one-quarter inch, Japanese manufacturers were producing parts with tolerances of one-sixteenth inch or less. The Japanese had built an amazing level of sophistication into their management systems by focusing the efforts of all employees toward creating products of high quality.

Where did the Japanese learn such innovative concepts? From American consultants. During the industrial boom of World War II, quality experts like W. Edwards Deming and Joseph M. Juran perfected their techniques and philosophies. In the late 1940s and early 1950s, Deming and Juran tried to spread the doctrine of improved productivity and profitability through quality management here in the United States but they were often met with a lukewarm reception. Many American businesspeople believed that quality and productivity were mutually exclusive terms. In other words, if one wanted high quality, productivity would naturally fall. Likewise, they believed that high levels of productivity caused lower quality. In the boom of the postwar years, most American businesspeople wanted no part of quality management.

Deming and Juran did find a receptive audience in postwar Japan. A series of lectures by both men in the early 1950s was a powerful catalyst for a remarkable transformation. Japanese businesses embraced the powerful paradigm of quality management, and slowly but surely the tide began to turn.

WHY IS QUALITY IMPORTANT?

The importance of quality can be summed up in a simple equation: less rework = higher productivity. Deming believed that many of the management techniques embraced in the West were counterintuitive. He believed that "measures of productivity do not lead to improvement in productivity." He also believed that something he referred to as "constancy of purpose for improvement of product and service" was an incredible catalyst that would galvanize an entire organization toward providing products and services that created devoted and enthusiastic customers. It may well be that Deming learned the importance of constancy of purpose while working with U.S. manufacturers during the 1940s and observing the remarkable results that were achieved by millions of Americans who were galvanized by the goal of winning the war. In the 1940s when resources were scarce, businesses understood the importance of reducing waste and conserving resources. During the economic boom that occurred after the end of World War II, most American manufacturers discarded the concepts of quality management that had been so crucial in winning the war against the Axis powers. The fact that Japan was able to rise from the ashes and challenge the economic dominance of the United States with concepts that were developed right here is one of the great ironies of all time.

One of the more important revelations of Deming's was the idea that all processes have a defined capability. Prior to Deming's revelation, managers believed that quality and production were the responsibility of each employee. Managers used threats, exhortations, and quotas to push workers to produce high levels of quality and production. This was based on the idea that the causes of most quality and production problems lie with the employee. Deming found quite the opposite to be true. In his experience he found that 94 percent of the causes of production problems were common causes. In other words, the causes of 94 percent of production problems were built into the process, and only management could resolve these issues.

WHAT IS A QUALITY MANAGEMENT SYSTEM?

All successful organizations must be managed as a system. Quality professionals like Deming and Juran believed that quality and customer satisfaction should be the focus of this system. Deming probably said it best in his book *Out of the Crisis*: "The customer is the most important part of the production line."

In Deming's view, the only reason for the existence of a company is to meet the needs of the customer. To be successful, organizations must understand the needs of their customers and must anticipate future needs. The job of every employee of the company is to ensure that customer requirements are met with the aim of exceeding expectations. Therefore, a quality management system is nothing more than a collection of policies, procedures, and resources that are developed, implemented, and continuously improved with the aims of determining the needs of the customer, allocating resources accordingly, and then controlling the various development processes in such a way that ensures high levels of product and/or service quality.

ISO 9001 simply provides requirements for the development of an effective quality management system. In implementing the requirements of the ISO 9001 standard to build your organization's quality management system, it is important that your employees understand the philosophy of quality management. An ISO 9001 quality management system shouldn't be a part of your management system—it should be the totality of your management system. To be effective, there must be no competition for resources between quality and productivity. Your managers must not believe that quality and productivity are a balancing act. Quality isn't everything; it's the only thing.

In *Out of the Crisis*, Deming tells a wonderful story about management at a furniture company who decided to expand into manufacturing pianos. The management team purchased the highest-quality piano currently being manufactured: a Steinway. The management team had the piano disassembled, and notes were taken of the design and arrangement of the various parts. The management team then made or bought different parts and put a piano together in the exact same manner as the Steinway. Unfortunately when the keys were struck, the piano produced nothing more than thuds. The team decided that manufacturing pianos was more difficult than they thought, so they decided to reassemble the Steinway with the intention to return the piano for a refund. After they reassembled the original parts, they were dismayed to discover that the Steinway too could now only produce thuds.

The lesson here is that we shouldn't copy the success of others. It is more important to learn the theory and philosophy behind successful organizations and then work to implement and improve upon them. If you try to implement the requirements of the ISO 9001 standard without adopting the philosophy of quality management, your management system will only produce thuds. The success of your quality management system requires a dramatic shift in the values of the organization. To be successful, your quality management system must not be merely compliant with the requirements of the ISO 9001 standard; it must be built on the principles of quality management.

The principles of quality management are the subject of the remainder of this book.

SUMMARY

- Many of the techniques and principles that Japan utilized to drastically increase market share in the 1980s and 1990s were developed right here in the United States.

- Quality management systems can improve productivity by reducing the amount of rework required.

- Processes have a defined capability. It is fruitless to continue using the same methods and expecting different results.

- Roughly 94 percent of the problems encountered are built into the process. Only management can eliminate the causes of these problems.

- To be successful, Deming believed that organizations must strive for a different bottom line: the satisfaction of the customer. ISO 9001 quality management systems are founded on the principle of customer satisfaction.

- Constancy of purpose is critical in the success of any organization.

- Understanding the philosophy of quality management systems is critical to a successful implementation.

- In order to successfully implement ISO 9001 in your organization, you must first seek to understand the philosophy of quality management.

3

ISO 9000 Family of Standards

If you think of "standardization" as the best you know
today, but which is to be improved tomorrow—you get
somewhere.

—Henry Ford, *Today and Tomorrow*

The story of ISO 9000 does not begin with quality management but rather with the issue of standardization. How important is standardization? Let me put it this way: without standardization, you couldn't read this book. Language was the first and the most important instance of standardization in human history. In order for human beings to communicate, agreement needed to be reached on the meaning of certain sounds. These standardized sounds became words. Through the development of words—both verbal and written—languages developed and civilization became possible. Standardization has become such a common part of our lives that we often take it for granted. After eating dinner at a restaurant, do you ever stop to wonder if your Visa card will work in this particular restaurant? When you send an e-mail to a new business contact from your HP personal computer, are you ever concerned that his Compaq may not be able to decode the data that is being transmitted? Of course you don't, but why not? How is this seamless integration of activities, machines, and organizations possible? The answer is international standards.

WHAT IS ISO?

Prior to World War II, there was very little standardization between European countries. This lack of standardization served as a barrier to free trade between different European countries and encouraged protectionist political policies, which had the effect of creating strong nationalistic sentiment within individual European nations. Because of this phenomenon, European countries remained isolated and fractured for many years. In the aftermath of World War II, many political leaders believed the key to bringing peace and prosperity to Europe lay in the emerging body of knowledge called standardization.

The International Organization for Standardization (ISO) was formed in 1947 by the consolidation of two international standards organizations: the International Federation of the National Standardizing Associations (ISA) and the United Nations Standards Coordinating Committee (UNSCC). The objective of the new organization was to "facilitate the international coordination and unification of industrial standards." ISO officially began operations on February 23, 1947, and set up their headquarters in Geneva, Switzerland. The founders of ISO were so committed to the concept of international standardization that they even went so far as to ensure that the name of the organization was standardized. The following text comes from the ISO Web site:

> Because "International Organization for Standardization" would have different acronyms in different languages ("IOS" in English, "OIN" in French for Organisation internationale de normalisation), its founders decided to give it also a short, all-purpose name. They chose "ISO," derived from the Greek isos, meaning "equal." Whatever the country, whatever the language, the short form of the organization's name is always ISO.

ISO is the international nerve center for standardization. Every country that participates in ISO has a member body in its own country. The member body for the United States is the American National Standards Institute (ANSI). ANSI works with other nations through ISO to develop and maintain international standards. ANSI also publishes ISO standards for use in the United States. ISO standards are developed and maintained by technical committees, which are composed of subject matter experts from sectors that requested the standards as well as representatives from academia, government organizations, and consumer associations. Once the standard is developed it is voted on by the national member bodies that participated in its development. In order for a new standard to be accepted, ISO bylaws require a two-thirds majority by all national member bodies that participated in the development of the standard and no more than 25 percent disapproval by all ISO members who vote on it. If you would like to learn more about the ISO system, visit their Web site (www.iso.org).

WHAT IS THE ISO 9000 FAMILY OF STANDARDS?

In 1979, ISO approved the formation of Technical Committee 176 (ISO/ TC 176). ISO/TC 176 was tasked with developing generic requirements for quality management systems that could be used across the globe. In 1987, ISO/TC 176 approved the first version of their new standard. ISO understood that this new standard would be significantly different from any other standard they had previously developed. ISO wanted to make a clear distinction for this exciting new direction for their organization so they wanted a unique designation for their newest standard. At the time, ISO was approaching 9000 published standards (they now have more than 17,500 standards in publication) so the organization decided to round up to 9000 for the new standard from ISO/TC 176 because round numbers are easier to remember. The ISO 9000 family of standards was born. The first version of the 9000 series included the following documents:

ISO 8402:1986 *Quality—Vocabulary*

ISO 9000:1987 *Quality management and quality assurance standards—Guidelines for selection and use*

ISO 9001:1987 *Quality systems—Model for quality assurance in design/development, production, installation and servicing*

ISO 9002:1987 *Quality systems—Model for quality assurance in production and installation*

ISO 9003:1987 *Quality systems—Model for quality assurance in final inspection and test*

ISO 9004:1987 *Quality management and quality system elements—Guidelines*

All the numbers may be a bit confusing to someone who doesn't understand the ISO numbering convention for standards. Figure 3.1 explains this convention.

The original series was successful but often criticized as being heavy on documentation and compliance, and light on process management. In 1994 the ISO 9000 series standards were revised. This revision saw some improvement but still maintained the "checklist" approach to compliance and certification. Customers of ISO 9000 were seeing substantial

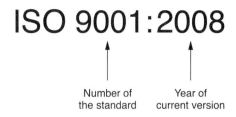

Figure 3.1   ISO numbering convention.

improvement but weren't realizing the concept of *continual* improvement, which formed the basis of so many of the teachings of Deming and Juran. In response to these concerns, ISO/TC 176 went back to the drawing board and redesigned the entire family of standards. On December 15, 2000, ISO released the ISO 9001:2000 standard.

WHAT IS ISO 9001?

In creating the ISO 9001:2000 standard, ISO/TC 176 significantly changed the structure of the ISO 9000 series. Instead of creating three separate documents that contained the requirements for quality management systems, ISO consolidated all requirements into one standard: ISO 9001. ISO greatly simplified the implementation of the standard by removing many of the documentation requirements and focusing the requirements on the concepts of customer satisfaction, process management, and continual improvement. On November 11, 2008, ISO revised the standard once again. The latest version of the ISO 9001 standard is ISO 9001:2008.

ISO 9001 contains generic requirements for the development of a quality management system. The requirements are intentionally vague so that they can be adapted for use in any organization regardless of size or complexity. A small service company with less than 50 employees can effectively implement a quality management system based on the same requirements as an exceedingly complex organization like Cisco Systems. In essence, the ISO 9001 standard doesn't tell organizations how to implement their quality management system—it simply documents what requirements must be met. This flexibility of the new, improved standard has arguably been the most important factor contributing to its success and worldwide acceptance over the past decade.

ISO 9001 is a "certifiable" standard, meaning that organizations who seek to provide increased assurance to their customers of their commitment to quality may seek certification of their management system from accredited third-party organizations. Certification is not necessary to obtain benefits from ISO 9001. Many organizations have used the requirements of the ISO 9001 standard to create robust quality management systems but have never bothered to obtain certification. The decision to pursue ISO 9001 certification should be based on a rigorous analysis of the organization's strategic goals and customer needs.

At the Illinois Department of Transportation, it was decided that certification could provide our agency with a greater appearance of transparency and would communicate our commitment to quality to our stakeholders in a manner that could not be otherwise achieved if we simply pursued compliance.

The certification process is explained in more detail in Chapter 15, "The Registrar."

OTHER MEMBERS OF THE FAMILY

The ISO 9000:2005 standard is an extremely important component of the ISO 9000 family. The ISO 9000:2005 standard contains important information that explains the fundamentals of quality management systems. Attempting to utilize ISO 9001 without the ISO 9000:2005 standard is like leaving for a vacation without a destination. You can use a map to navigate the roads, but if you don't know where you are going, what's the point? The ISO 9000:2005 standard contains a wonderful description of your destination and provides definitions for the terminology you'll need to get there. The ISO 9000:2005 standard also contains the eight quality management principles that form the basis of the ISO 9001 standard (as well as the basis of this book!).

The ISO 9004:2000 standard contains guidelines for performance improvements. Once your organization has achieved compliance with the ISO 9001 standard requirements, ISO 9004:2000 can be a valuable tool to help you improve your organization's quality management system. Furthermore, the ISO 9004:2000 standard contains additional language that can help you better understand the intent of the ISO 9001 standard. This can be extremely valuable as you work to determine the best means of implementing the ISO 9001 standard requirements within your organization.

The ISO 9000:2005 and ISO 9004:2000 standards are not intended to be used as the basis for certification.

DO I HAVE TO BUY A BUNCH OF COPIES OF THE ISO 9000 STANDARDS FOR ALL OF MY EMPLOYEES?

The answer is no. Your employees do not need to know the requirements of the ISO 9001 standard. They need to understand the requirements of your organization's quality management system. In order to be certified to the ISO 9001 standard, your organization's quality management system must meet all the requirements of the ISO 9001 standard.

SUMMARY

- ISO is the international abbreviation for the International Organization for Standardization in Geneva, Switzerland.

- The ISO 9000 family is a group of standards that provides generic guidelines for the establishment of a quality management system within an organization.

- ISO 9000:2005 contains the fundamentals of quality management systems and provides guidance on vocabulary.

- ISO 9004:2000 contains guidelines for performance improvements to existing quality management systems.

- Certification is not a requirement of ISO 9001. Many organizations choose to adopt the ISO 9001 requirements but do not opt to pursue certification.

- ISO 9004:2000 is not intended to be used as a basis for third-party certification but rather provides guidance for organizations looking to move their systems beyond compliance toward continual improvement.

- ISO 9001 is a blueprint for the construction of your organization's quality management system. It doesn't tell you *how* to do it; it simply tells you what requirements must be met.

- It's nice if your employees understand the requirements of ISO 9001, but it's essential that your employees understand how the organization's quality management system works.

4

ISO 9001
Certification Process

*The wise man belongs to all countries, for the home of a
great soul is the whole world.*

—Democritus

INTRODUCTION

In my experience with ISO 9001, I have found that most people assume that
ISO certifies organizations to the standard. This is not the case. ISO doesn't
certify any product, service, or organization to any of their standards. If
you decide to pursue certification of your quality management system, then
there are a few things you need to understand about the certification process. At the Illinois Department of Transportation (IDOT), we got lucky in
that we had a good relationship with a major consulting firm who referred
us to an excellent certification organization. Looking back now, I can see
that we were extremely fortunate to have found a good partner, but I can
also see that we took on some risks in not doing our homework. Fortunately
for us, things worked out well. This chapter is very important, so don't
skip through it. There are some important concepts you need to understand
before you begin your ISO journey. Don't take unnecessary risks in this
area. Take the time to understand all the issues associated with certification and do your homework to ensure that you find the best match for your
organization. Most importantly, you need to remember that ISO 9001 is a
global standard. If you make the decision to pursue certification, you'll be
stepping up to bat in the big leagues. In many ways, the whole world will
be watching you from this point on, so you need to understand the international system that has developed to provide consistency in the certification process.

DO WE HAVE TO BE CERTIFIED?

First of all, it is important that you understand that certification to the ISO 9001 standard is not necessary to realize benefits for your organization. As mentioned previously, many organizations use the standard as a foundation for the development of an effective management system but do not pursue certification. For organizations who desire to demonstrate a higher level of accountability and assurance, the decision to pursue ISO 9001 certification can be an excellent means of improving the level of conformance to the requirements of the standard.

WHAT IS THE CERTIFICATION PROCESS?

Certification services are provided by independent third-party organizations. Auditors from certification bodies (registrars) review the organization's management system to determine its level of conformance to the requirements of the ISO 9001 standard. ISO 9001 certification consists of a number of reviews of your organization's quality management system. In most cases, it is a five-step process (see Figure 4.1).

The first review is a desk audit of your documentation. This is typically conducted off-site at the auditor's facility. The organization submits their documentation to the auditor and it is reviewed to determine the level of conformance to the documentation requirements of the ISO 9001 standard. If there are no major issues, the next step is an on-site readiness review

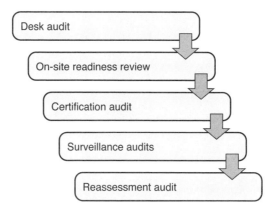

Figure 4.1 ISO 9001 certification process.

(ORR). During the ORR the auditor samples several processes within the scope of the organization's quality management system to determine if the organization is ready for a full certification audit. If no major issues are identified during the ORR, the next step is the certification audit. The certification audit involves a review of all of the processes and areas identified in the scope of the organization's quality manual. The auditor does not have the ultimate say in determining whether or not an organization will be certified. The auditor can only make a recommendation. A separate certification board within the certification body reviews the recommendation of the auditor and makes the final decision. If the audit team finds the level of conformance to be acceptable, the audit team will make a recommendation for certification to the certification board.

ISO 9001 certification agreements are typically three-year contracts. Surveillance audits are required on at least an annual basis. At IDOT we chose to do biannual surveillance audits, which means we split our annual audit into two separate audits per year. At the end of the three-year certification period, the organization must undergo a reassessment audit. The reassessment audit is similar in scope to the certification audit although that can be the subject of some negotiation. If conformance to the standard has been high during previous audits, the scope of the reassessment audit can be a great deal smaller than that of the original certification audit.

WHAT IS ACCREDITATION?

ISO recognizes the practice of certification for the ISO 9001 standard and has provided an international standard (ISO 17021) to document requirements for bodies providing audit and certification of management systems. Implementation of this standard allows for *accreditation* of certifying bodies. According to ISO, accreditation means that "a certification body has been officially approved as competent to carry out certification in specified business sectors by a national accreditation body." It's important to note that accreditation is voluntary in most countries, including the United States. In my estimation, choosing a certification body that is accredited doesn't ensure that you will find a great registrar, but it will increase your chances dramatically.

In 1993, the International Accreditation Forum (IAF) was formed with the primary objective of developing ". . . a single, worldwide program of conformity assessment, which reduces risks for business and end users by ensuring that accredited certificates and certifications may be relied upon." The IAF certification process is an intricate system of checks and balances that help ensure that standards are interpreted and implemented similarly

Figure 4.2 IAF accrediation process.

worldwide. Through the use of Multilateral Recognition Arrangements (MLAs) with member national accreditation bodies, the IAF has streamlined the certification process. An organization that is certified to an international standard by an accredited certifying body will have its certification accepted by all nations covered within the MLA. It is the goal of IAF that all organizations can be "certified once, accepted everywhere" by choosing certifying bodies that have been accredited. One of the requirements of IAF accreditation is compliance with the requirements of the ISO 17011 standard (*Conformity assessment—General requirements for accreditation bodies accrediting conformity assessment bodies*). The benefits of choosing an accredited certification body are similar to the benefits you realize when choosing an ISO 9001–certified company. If you receive a referral to a certification body, you should contact the national accreditation body in your country to ensure that the organization is properly accredited. See Figure 4.2. The IAF provides a list of national accreditation bodies on their Web site (www.iaf.nu).

WHAT ARE THE PROS AND CONS OF ISO 9001 CERTIFICATION?

ISO 9001 certification can provide your organization with many benefits, including improved conformance to documented procedures and more

Table 4.1 Pros and cons of ISO 9001 certification.

Pros	Cons
Independent third-party verification provides assurance that requirements have been correctly interpreted and implemented	Additional costs in time and money
Successful certification can be a source of pride for the organization	Continual surveillance audits required
Certification can provide additional assurance to stakeholders	Depending on your current operating system, more documentation may be necessary to conform to the standard
Cost savings are often realized from corrective actions implemented as a result of audit findings	Requires many records to be maintained to demonstrate conformance of the system

effective implementation of the ISO 9001 standard requirements, but there can be significant costs that accompany certification. Table 4.1 summarizes some of the pros and cons of ISO 9001 certification.

The decision to pursue certification should be based on an analysis of business needs and a determination of whether or not certification will help the organization more effectively accomplish its mission.

USING YOUR ISO 9001 CERTIFICATION FOR PUBLIC AWARENESS

Most certification bodies have very specific requirements for the use of your certification mark. The ISO trademark may not be used at any time by your organization in connection with the certification of your management system. Most certification bodies will allow you to use their certification mark for publicizing your ISO 9001 certification. Your certification specialist should be able to provide you access to the mark as well as requirements for its use once your management system has been certified. These requirements will vary between certification bodies but most will likely enforce the following rules:

- The certification mark should not state that a product or service is "ISO 9001 certified."

- Use of the certification mark should only state "management system registered to ISO 9001."

- The mark may be used on sales literature, marketing materials, and technical publications but not in conjunction with any product or service in a manner that implies certification of the product/service.

- All literature bearing the mark of the certification body must indicate the date of printing.

Additionally, ISO provides the following guidelines for publicizing the certification of your management system:

- Use "ISO 9001 certified" not "ISO certified" when referring to your certification.

- Be accurate and concise about the scope of your management system certification in all public releases. A reader should be able to understand exactly what areas of the organization's management system are certified.

- You may create your own mark using the symbol of your organization so long as it is not designed in such a way as to be interpreted as ISO's logo.

SUMMARY

- ISO does not provide certification services for any of its standards.

- Third-party certification is not required to benefit from use of the ISO 9001 standard in your organization.

- Organizations that desire a higher level of confidence can pursue certification through the use of accredited third-party certification bodies.

- The decision to pursue ISO 9001 certification should be based on an analysis of the organization's strategy and goals.

- ISO 9001 certification is performed by independent third-party organizations.

- If you wish to pursue third-party certification, you need to do your homework.

- If you receive a referral to a certification body, you should contact the national accreditation body in your country to ensure that the organization is properly accredited. The IAF provides a list of national accreditation bodies on their Web site (www.iaf.nu).

- Some certification organizations are not accredited with the ANSI–ASQ National Accreditation Board (ANAB). It is not recommended that you utilize these firms for your certification.

- Additional discussion regarding the certification process is provided in Chapter 15.

- ISO 9001 certification can be an excellent marketing tool for your organization, but there are some very specific guidelines to the use of your organization's certification mark.

5

Eight Quality Management Principles

The value of a principle is the number of things it will explain.

—Ralph Waldo Emerson

INTRODUCTION

Have you ever witnessed a professional golf tournament? The skill that these players possess is truly remarkable. The timing, hand–eye coordination, and precision required to re-create a world-class golf swing are possessed by very few individuals. If you were to watch an analysis of the golf swings of several different professional golfers, you'd find that every golfer has a unique style, yet there are certain things that they all do exactly the same. We call these things *fundamentals*. Another way to say it is that there are certain universal principles that form the basis of a good golf swing.

The fundamentals are equally important in business as they are in the world of golf. All organizations are unique, yet in order to be successful there are certain universal principles that they must adopt and observe. At the Illinois Department of Transportation, we struggled to understand the proper interpretation of the ISO 9001 standard requirements for many months. As we attempted to interpret these requirements and make them relevant to our operations, I was often reminded of the computer-generated 3-D posters that were so popular in the 1990s. Like those 3-D posters, we'd stare and stare at the standard requirements for hours until a pattern would begin to emerge. Just as we were about the see the picture, we'd become distracted and the image would fade away. This process continued for many months as we worked to build our management system. In order to see the image in a 3-D poster, a certain perspective is required. One must look beyond the individual components of the puzzle to see the picture. The same can be said of the ISO 9001 standard requirements. In order to fully understand how to implement the requirements, one must look at them from the perspective of the fundamentals.

EIGHT QUALITY MANAGEMENT PRINCIPLES OF ISO 9000:2005

It should come as no surprise that the ISO 9001 standard was written based on a thorough understanding of the fundamentals of quality management. These fundamentals are known as the *eight quality management principles* and they are found in the ISO 9000:2005 standard *Quality management systems—Fundamentals and vocabulary.* ISO 9000:2005 explains the fundamentals of quality management and provides a glossary with definitions for some of the unique vocabulary found in quality management. These principles are intended to be used by senior management as a framework to guide their organizations toward improved performance:

1. *Customer focus.* Organizations depend on their customers and therefore should understand current and future customer needs, meet customer requirements, and strive to exceed customer expectations.

2. *Leadership.* Leaders establish unity of purpose and direction of the organization. They should create and maintain an internal environment in which people can become truly involved in achieving the organization's objectives.

3. *Involvement of people,* People at all levels are the essence of an organization, and their full involvement enables their abilities to be used for the organization's benefit.

4. *Process approach.* A desired result is achieved more efficiently when activities and related resources are managed as a process.

5. *System approach to management.* Identifying, understanding, and managing interrelated processes as a system contributes to the organization's effectiveness and efficiency in achieving its objectives.

6. *Continual improvement.* Continual improvement of the organization's overall performance should be a permanent objective of the organization.

7. *Factual approach to decision making.* Effective decisions are based on the analysis of data and information.

8. *Mutually beneficial supplier relationships.* An organization and its suppliers are interdependent, and a mutually beneficial relationship enhances the ability of both to create value.

The leadership guru Stephen Covey believes there are universal principles that are just as real and important as natural laws. In the same manner that natural laws form the foundation of all breakthroughs in the physical sciences, universal principles should form the basis of our management theories. In Covey's estimation, organizations that seek to thrive in today's fast-paced business environment must align their activities with strong principles that will hold the organization together through the violent storms of the normal business cycles. Any organization can thrive when the business environment is favorable, but only organizations that understand the importance of universal principles such as customer satisfaction and continual improvement will survive the tough times.

A great example of an organization that embraces universal principles is the Toyota Motor Corporation. The recent fascination with the Toyota Production System has spawned hundreds of books focused on identifying the procedures and policies the Toyota Motor Corporation has adopted in their phenomenally successful management system. Though well intentioned, most of these attempts to unlock the mysteries of Toyota's success miss the boat. Toyota's success lies in the creation and adherence to fundamental organizational principles. If you wish to mirror Toyota's success, you need adopt Toyota's principles—not necessarily their policies and procedures. Similarly, if you wish to build a successful ISO 9001 quality management system, begin by using the eight quality management principles in your own organization.

BRIDGING THE GAP BETWEEN STRATEGY AND EXECUTION

It's a dirty little secret in organizational management that middle managers have the most difficult job in the entire organization. Top management must attempt to peer ahead and see the threats and opportunities that await the organization in the future. Their job is to develop a strategy that mitigates the impact of potential threats while exploiting opportunities to the maximum extent possible. Frontline employees are responsible for implementing the organization's strategy. Middle management has the unenviable task of analyzing the high-level goals and objectives of the executive strategy and translating them into tasks and initiatives that frontline employees can strive to achieve. This can be exceedingly difficult. Your organization may

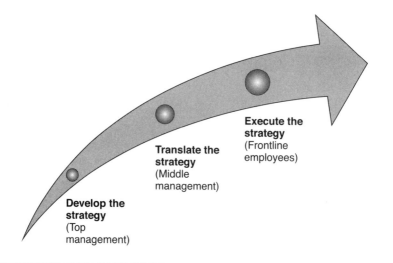

Execute the
strategy
(Frontline
employees)

Translate the
strategy
(Middle
management)

Develop the
strategy
(Top
management)

Figure 5.1   Steps in the strategic planning process.

possess a talented executive staff and a world-class workforce, but if middle management can not adequately translate the organization's strategy into specific targets and goals, the strategy will fail. Organizations that do not understand this phenomenon often encounter what I call an "execution gap" in their strategic planning process. See Figure 5.1.

The execution gap most often occurs at the level of middle management because of an inability to interpret the strategy into action items. Most often, the problem comes down to a lack of principles within the organization. When carefully chosen and effectively implemented, principles create an invisible guiding force that aligns the efforts and activities of the entire organization toward the achievement of strategic goals. Just as a compass can guide a hiker through the wilderness by use of the powerful magnetic fields that surround the earth, an employee can use the framework of a principle-centered quality management system (QMS) to guide their day-to-day actions.

Securing the understanding of middle managers is often the most important component in the successful implementation of an ISO 9001 quality management system. The eight quality management principles are critical to the successful implementation of your quality management system because they are easy to understand and will be readily embraced by your employees. Use of these principles creates a "Rosetta Stone" for your middle managers that will allow them to translate the generic requirements of the ISO 9001 standard into language each employee can understand, as in the following examples:

> "Review of requirements related to the product/service is important because we want to maintain a customer focus in our organization."

> "An effective management review process is critical to our success because we want to manage our organization as a system rather than as a loose collection of independent departments."

By adopting the eight quality management principles of ISO 9000:2005 as the framework of your ISO 9001 quality management system, you will build a solid foundation for the future success of your organization. When the storms of change rage and the latest management fads are swept away, the eight quality management principles will provide refuge and direction for your employees. These critical principles form the basis of the remainder of this book.

SUMMARY

- In order to be successful, organizations must develop and adopt principles to guide the actions and decisions of all employees.

- In order to achieve high levels of quality, there are certain universal principles that must be implemented in all organizations, regardless of the type or application.

- The eight quality management principles form the basis for the requirements of the ISO 9001 standard.

- Securing the understanding of middle managers is often the most important component in the successful implementation of an ISO 9001 quality management system.

- The framework of the eight quality management standards can be an excellent tool to improve understanding and implementation of ISO 9001 requirements by your employees.

- The analysis of each quality management principle within the framework of the ISO 9001 standard forms the bulk of the remainder of this book.

6

Customer Focus

INTRODUCTION

All organizations—even public-sector organizations—are created to fill the needs and requirements of customers, yet a breakdown in the understanding of this concept seems to occur within government organizations. In the minds of many public-sector employees, the operating budgets of government agencies do not appear to be directly affected by the choices of customers in the same manner as they are in the private sector. Additionally, the highly specialized work and the absence of adequate alignment of organizational objectives and goals throughout public-sector organizations often isolate government employees from their customers. This mind-set leads to a vicious cycle of decreasing employee engagement and increasing customer dissatisfaction. In a recent Gallup poll, only 26 percent of Americans indicated they had a great deal or fair amount of trust in the way the nation is being governed. Customers of public-sector organizations seem to be saying, "Why can't you be good to me?"

THE CUSTOMER IS ALWAYS RIGHT

In 1909 a man by the name of Harry Gordon Selfridge opened a huge department store in London named Selfridges. Selfridge had cut his teeth in retailing under the tutorage of the legendary Marshall Field, and during this time he had learned the importance of excellent customer service.

Shortly after opening his new store, Selfridge created the famous slogan "the customer is always right" and used it extensively to advertise the high quality and service of his stores. During the course of the past 100 years, this phrase has worked its way into conventional wisdom. Mr. Selfridge's idiom was an extremely clever tool for differentiating his store from those of his competitors, but it is doubtful that he ever intended for this slogan to become a fundamental law of business. Unfortunately, many people believe that blind obedience to the whims of each customer is essential to the survival of an organization.

This approach—"the customer is always right"—suggests that the customer must determine what it is he or she wants from the organization. Certainly this is an important part of the equation but, unfortunately, it's a very small part of a larger picture. The best organizations don't focus on customer *wants*; they work very hard to understand current and future customer *needs*. A lesser-known quote attributed to Gordon Selfridge probably better captures the true essence of a customer focus: "People will sit up and take notice of you if you will sit up and take notice of what makes them sit up and take notice." Though not quite as elegant as its more famous cousin, this quote better captures the challenges facing a customer-focused organization. In order to be successful, top management in *all* organizations must expend the time and energy required to figure out what will make their customers "sit up and take notice."

CLAUSE 5.2: CUSTOMER FOCUS

Clause 5.2 of the ISO 9001 standard requires that top management ensure that customer requirements are met with the aim of enhancing customer satisfaction. Achieving true customer focus in an organization requires a shift in culture. The objective of enhancing customer satisfaction should be a major objective of the organization's strategy. At the Illinois Department of Transportation we really struggled with the concept of "customers." Many of our employees believed that achieving a customer focus simply wasn't possible within the environment of a public-sector agency. Furthermore, many employees told us that we *shouldn't* be treating taxpayers as customers because we had a statutory mandate to make decisions for the overall good of the traveling public. Anyone who travels on an Illinois highway is technically a customer of IDOT. How can any organization—public or private—manage such a wide, diverse customer base? At IDOT, we discovered that the key to implementing a customer focus in a government agency is a matter of maintaining the proper perspective.

In Illinois, IDOT is an agency of the executive wing of a representative government. Illinois residents elect representatives to communicate their needs and requirements and to act in their best interests. In this way, elected officials are like a focus group that defines and communicates customer requirements through the legislative process. The governor's office works with legislative representatives to determine high-level customer requirements and defines those requirements into priorities and objectives for the agency to achieve. To achieve customer focus, IDOT management must translate those priorities and objectives into a vision and mission for the organization. The mission and vision are then used to determine a quality policy and quality objectives to drive fulfillment of customer requirements and continual improvement of the agency's processes. The quality objectives must be driven from the highest levels in the organization all the way down to the employees on the front lines. Thus, the key to establishing a customer focus is an effective strategic plan that cascades overall strategic objectives into specific quality objectives for each employee to achieve.

CLAUSE 7.2.1: DETERMINATION OF REQUIREMENTS RELATED TO THE PRODUCT/SERVICE

Clause 7.2.1 of the ISO 9001 standard requires the organization to determine:

a) requirements specified by the customer,

b) requirements not stated by the customer but necessary for specified or intended use, where known,

c) statutory and regulatory requirements related to the product/ service, and

d) any additional requirements determined by the organization

In order to meet this requirement, an organization should develop a formal process for determining and documenting all requirements for a given product or service. The output of this process is an important input into the planning of product/service realization (clause 7.1). This output can be documented in many different ways. The methodology employed isn't important so long as a comprehensive assessment is completed to determine all of the different requirements of the product or service. Remember that quality is defined by the ISO 9001 standard as the degree to which a set of inherent characteristics fulfills requirements. Quality can not be measured unless all the requirements are known.

CLAUSE 7.2.2: REVIEW OF REQUIREMENTS RELATED TO THE PRODUCT/SERVICE

Clause 7.2.2 of the ISO 9001 standard requires the organization to review the requirements related to the product/service prior to the organization's commitment to supply the product/service to the customer. The intent of this requirement is to ensure that all the necessary product/service requirements have been determined, that all outstanding issues involving the product/service have been resolved, and that the organization can indeed meet all of the defined requirements. Records of this review are required to be maintained.

IDOT'S EXPERIENCE

In public service agencies, there are often two levels of customer requirements: the program level and the project level. This is certainly true at IDOT. We have two different levels for determining requirements: the program level and the project level.

PROGRAM-LEVEL REQUIREMENTS

The great majority of our projects utilize federal funding. These federal funds are tied to programs that have specific requirements and limitations for use. When new programs are developed or existing programs are revised, the Department must analyze the program requirements to develop guidelines for the use of these funds. The most recent federal program that required this type of review was the American Recovery and Reinvestment Act (ARRA) of 2009. This program distributed nearly $50 billion dollars to rebuild America's transportation system. Illinois received an allotment of nearly $1 billion for state and local road and bridge projects alone. The ARRA was president Barack Obama's response to the recession of 2008–2009 and therefore represented an important area of focus for IDOT. The president's home state was expected to lead the way for the rest of the country.

We began first at the program level. We needed to review ARRA to identify the many requirements related to this new federal program. Once the requirements were determined, we documented them in an ARRA quality plan. Due to the importance of the ARRA, it was determined that a separate quality plan would be needed to ensure effective implementation and control of ARRA funds. This quality plan would document all of the requirements of the ARRA and would serve as a record of the actions our agency completed to administer this historic program. Figure 6.1 outlines these various steps; as an example, Table 6.1 shows the program-level requirements of the American Recovery and Reinvestment Act of 2009.

PROJECT-LEVEL REQUIREMENTS

Once the requirements of the ARRA were documented in our quality plan, we then needed to identify requirements for individual projects. This was accomplished by determining an appropriate scope for the project: rehabilitation, reconstruction, resurfacing, or new construction. The determination of the scope of the project is a delicate balancing act that requires IDOT to incorporate the needs of the public, the priorities of the governor's office, the demands of the legislature, and a thorough analysis of existing and future traffic patterns into the decision. After the scope of the project

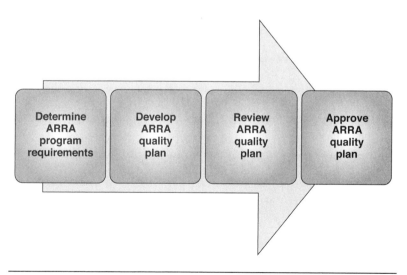

Figure 6.1   Determination and review of requirements—program level.

Table 6.1 Program-level requirements example—ARRA program.

American Recovery and Reinvestment Act of 2009

Element	Requirements
Funding criteria	• Projects must be "shovel ready" • Priority must be given to economically depressed areas • Projects must be completed within two years
Purchasing requirements	• Domestic iron and steel must be used for all ARRA projects • Disadvantaged Business Enterprise provisions of SAFETEA-LU apply
Reporting requirements	• 1201, 1511, and 1607 certifications required • Monthly employment summary • Monthly progress report
Special requirements	• Special signing required • Process for public submission of projects required

is determined, the real work begins. Impacts to environmental and cultural resources resulting from the project must be identified and mitigated to satisfy federal requirements, the need for land acquisition and utility adjustments must be determined, and timing and cost constraints must be established. Once all project requirements are determined, they are documented in a project report. This document summarizes all the requirements of an individual project and serves as the input into our design process. The review and approval of the project report concludes the process of determination of requirements related to the product/service required by the ISO 9001 standard. Figure 6.2 outlines these various steps; as an example, Table 6.2 shows the project-level requirements of the ARRA.

When projects are determined to have a significant impact to the surrounding community, IDOT uses an approach called *context sensitive solutions* (CSS). CSS is an outreach and collaboration process that helps IDOT provide cost-effective transportation facilities that add lasting value to the communities it serves. Before CSS, IDOT would develop a design for each major project and then conduct a public meeting to review the design. Often the time frame left little time for design changes to be made if public

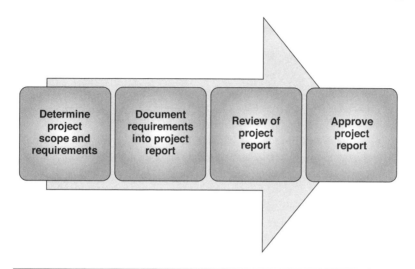

Figure 6.2 Determination and review of requirements—project level.

Table 6.2 Project-level requirements example—ARRA project.

ARRA Project

Element	Requirements
Environmental/cultural coordination	• Erosion control plan required • Mitigation plan required for endangered species within project limits • Trenching not allowed outside of existing right-of-way
Utility coordination	• Water main adjustment required • 30″ sanitary sewer not to be disturbed • City engineer to be notified at least two weeks prior to project start-up
Funding requirements	• Project cost = $3,000,000 (ARRA—100% federal) • Utility relocation = $250,000 (100% state) • Land acquisition = $30,000 (100% state)
Contract requirements	• ARRA signing special provision required • ARRA project reporting special provision required • August 31, 2010 completion date

acceptance of the plan was low. This resulted in one of two outcomes: 1) forced acceptance of an unpopular project proposal, or 2) costly redesign. Neither alternative was a desirable outcome.

The focus of CSS is to identify specific customer concerns and requirements during the preliminary design stage. Once we implemented CSS, we found that implementing a customer focus actually saved IDOT time and money by integrating specific customer concerns and requirements into the preliminary design. Instead of costly redesigns that added months to the project schedule, IDOT was able to integrate customer concerns and specific requirements into the project design early in the process. This has made IDOT more responsive to customer needs and more efficient at the same time.

CLAUSE 7.2.3: CUSTOMER COMMUNICATION

Clause 7.2.3 of the ISO 9001 standard requires that organizations determine and implement effective arrangements for communicating with customers in relation to product information, enquiries, contracts or order handling, including amendments, and customer feedback, including customer complaints. At IDOT, this was accomplished in a variety of ways: through the use of the agency's Web site, toll-free phone lines, e-mail, brochures, and public outreach events. For IDOT, satisfying this requirement helped improve the transparency of our organization immensely. The ISO 9001 standard doesn't specifically require a customer complaint log, but for some reason most registrars require one. In order to satisfy this requirement, we created a simple Access database so the employees in our communication center can create a record when complaints are received. A supervisor reviews each record, and that supervisor determines the need for any follow-up activities.

Use of the database allows us to review the overall process from time to time by analyzing the data to determine the frequency of the different types of complaints. We found these data to be very useful in determining the need to implement corrective action. One of our overall objectives is to reduce the number of complaints from our customers. Our customer complaint database was created in 2003, and during the first year we recorded 615 separate complaints. By 2007 that number had been reduced to 196.

CLAUSE 8.2.1: CUSTOMER SATISFACTION

Clause 8.2.1 of the ISO 9001 standard requires the organization to develop a method for monitoring information relating to customer perception as to whether the organization has met customer requirements. In order to address this requirement, IDOT created a comprehensive survey that is administered to Illinois motorists annually. This survey contains a multitude of questions that help us gauge the perceptions and attitudes of the traveling public. The results of the survey are an important input into our management review process. By studying the results and working to identify trends in perception and satisfaction, IDOT has been able to make adjustments to our strategic plan and deployment of resources in order to better satisfy our customers.

Achieving a customer focus in a public-sector organization is much easier when organizational and individual goals are aligned with an effective strategic plan. Implementation of the ISO 9001 standard can help your organization enforce a customer focus by providing the framework necessary to develop effective processes for determining customer requirements and ensuring overall customer satisfaction.

SUMMARY

- All organizations have customers—even public-sector organizations.

- Overspecialization and absence of adequate alignment of organizational and individual objectives and goals often isolates public-sector employees from their customers.

- To be successful, organizations must work hard to understand current and future customer needs.

- The key to implementing a customer focus in a public-sector organization is a matter of maintaining the proper focus.

- Quality can not be measured unless all the necessary requirements are known.

- In many public-sector organizations there exist two levels for determining customer requirements: the program level and the project level.

- In order to achieve certification of your management system, your organization will need to develop and implement a customer complaint log.

- A customer survey is an effective way to satisfy the requirements of clause 8.2.1 (customer satisfaction).

7

Leadership

A very great vision is needed, and the man who has it must follow it as the eagle seeks the deepest blue of the sky.

—Crazy Horse

When we first began this journey, my son and I took a summer vacation to Washington D.C. On the last evening of our trip, we visited the Lincoln Memorial. I was surprised to find the Lincoln Memorial to be a moving testament to the power of leadership. Daniel Chester French was the remarkable sculptor who created the main statue of the Memorial, and he worked hard to capture the essence of Lincoln's leadership style.

When viewing the statue from the front of the monument, it looks impressive but somewhat unremarkable. It's just another large statue of a famous politician in a city where such tributes are a dime a dozen. It's not until you walk behind the statue that the symbolism that Daniel Chester French worked so hard to sculpt into his masterpiece comes alive. From the back of the statue, you realize that Lincoln is staring at the Washington Monument—our nation's most enduring symbol of unity. The statue perfectly captures Abraham Lincoln's vision of a truly United States: not a loose confederation of sovereign states, not two countries separated by a line that marked north and south.

If you look carefully at the statue, you'll see that Lincoln's left hand is closed in a fist—this signifies resolve. Abraham Lincoln stubbornly persisted with his vision in the face of eroding public support for the war, intense pressure from a bitter, hostile legislature, and even resistance from his own cabinet. In 1863, it looked like all hope was lost for the war effort, and the possibility of a second term for Lincoln seemed remote at best. Yet

Lincoln stood fast. The more difficult the effort became, the more stubbornly Lincoln held on to his vision for the country. Abraham Lincoln had a vision for the United States, and it did not include a North and a South. Though it ultimately cost him his life, Abraham Lincoln stuck by that vision through good times and bad, and the world is a much different place 144 years later.

Effective leadership in any organization requires a mixture of clear vision and stern resolve. Successful organizations are composed of leaders who can define a vision for the organization and then realize that vision through the sheer force of their collective will. Through their collective vision, they can transform a loose confederation of sovereign departments into a cohesive, high-performing team. The ISO 9001 standard recognizes the importance of leadership and contains some very specific requirements for top management.

At the Illinois Department of Transportation, we understood the importance of management commitment to improvement initiatives. Because of this, we were especially diligent when designing our quality management system to ensure that management responsibilities were sufficiently defined within our documented procedures to produce the momentum needed to push the ISO 9001 certification program to all areas of the organization.

MANAGEMENT COMMITMENT

Clause 5.1 of the ISO 9001 standard requires top management to provide evidence of its commitment to the development and implementation of the QMS. There are five main requirements that must be met. Top management must:

1. Communicate the importance of meeting requirements (customer and statutory/regulatory)

2. Establish and communicate a quality policy throughout the organization

3. Ensure that objectives are established in relevant areas

4. Conduct management reviews at specified intervals

5. Ensure that resources are allocated effectively based on demonstrated need

The first requirement is truly the most important one. At IDOT our employees look to the secretary of transportation to set their priorities. If ISO 9001 is a priority, then the secretary must speak about it everywhere he goes. He must find opportunities to inject ISO 9001 into the conversation whenever and wherever possible. If employees hear the secretary talk about it often, they will make it a priority in their day-to-day activities. If top management does not speak about ISO 9001 as much as possible, employees will decide that it's not a priority and they will quickly lose interest.

It's extremely important to build management commitment into a management system. The ISO 9001 standard provides specific requirements needed to achieve the level of engagement necessary to ensure that customer requirements are met with the aim of enhancing customer satisfaction. Conformance to these requirements will certainly yield excellent results, but if the goal of the organization is to become one of those rare, bright stars, management must make a concerted effort to move beyond compliance and strive for excellence. What follows is our attempt to use the minimum requirements of the ISO 9001 standard as a springboard to achieve world-class performance.

QUALITY POLICY AND QUALITY OBJECTIVES

Clause 4.2.1(a) of the ISO 9001 standard requires the organization to establish documented statements of a quality policy and quality objectives. Clause 5.3 and clause 5.4.1 contain the requirements for the quality policy and quality objectives. It's important to note that the quality policy must include a commitment to comply with requirements and to continually improve the effectiveness of the management system, and the quality objectives must be measurable and consistent with the quality policy. These requirements are no accident. From an organizational perspective, the quality policy is a document that explains to everyone what we do and why we do it.

Stephen Covey wrote in *The 7 Habits of Highly Effective People* that successful people begin with the end in mind. This is the approach we took in the establishment of a quality policy and overall quality objectives. We believed that the implementation of the ISO 9001 standard would be most effective if it were directly tied to our strategic plan. Our strategic plan identifies our destination; it shows us where we need to go. We tied the quality policy directly to the vision and mission of the organization, as shown in Figure 7.1.

The quality policy defines what quality means to us: we will meet customer requirements and exceed expectations wherever possible. We were pleased with our quality policy, but we decided that we needed to condense the wording of the policy into something simple that each employee could remember each day as they completed their responsibilities. To accomplish

---

Our Vision

The Illinois Department of Transportation will be recognized as the premier state department of transportation in the nation.

Our Mission

We provide safe, cost-effective transportation for Illinois in ways that enhance quality of life, promote economic prosperity, and demonstrate respect for our environment.

Our Guiding Principles

We will accomplish our mission while making the following principles the hallmark of all our work:

Safety · Integrity · Responsiveness · Quality · Innovation

Quality Policy

IDOT will consistently provide safe, cost-effective transportation for Illinois that meets or exceeds the requirements and expectations of our customers. We will actively pursue ever-improving quality through programs that enable each employee to do the job right the first time, every time.

Figure 7.1 Tying the quality policy to IDOT's mission.

this goal, we created a quality statement that sums up in eight short words what each employee needs to do to implement the quality policy:

Do it right the first time, every time.

From our perspective, the quality policy and the quality statement define what quality means for the entire organization. Instead of explaining the ISO 9001 requirements to our employees, we concentrated instead on explaining the quality policy and quality statement to them at every opportunity. We tried to work the quality policy and quality statement into every presentation, every meeting, every conversation.

Our quality objectives were drawn from the agency's strategic plan and represented broad, organization-wide targets and goals. The quality objectives define success for us.

They allow us to measure our progress and determine when changes may need to be made. They also provide a platform for the establishment of more-specific objectives in all areas of the Department.

We understood that in order to be successful, we must define the terms of success. Our registrar likes to ask the question, "If I ran into success on the street, how would I recognize him?" I believe this is a great question to ask of every organization. What does success mean to you? How will you know when you have achieved it? Most importantly, how can you

---

Outcome 1: Improved safety on roads and bridges

Quality objective 1: Reduce fatalities on the Illinois State Highway System to no more than 1000 by January 1, 2009.

Outcome 2: Improved planning and programming of road and bridge improvements

Quality objective 2: Plan and program projects in annual and multiyear programs to ensure that at least 85 percent of all state highways and bridges remain in acceptable condition.

Outcome 3: Improved project design estimates

Quality objective 3: Limit the difference between project estimates and contract awards to an average of no more than 5 percent for all projects.

Quality objective 4: Limit construction contract change orders to 5 percent or less of the contract award amount.

Outcome 4: Improved delivery of construction programs

Quality objective 5: Obligate at least 95 percent of available construction funds to projects outlined in the annual program.

Quality objective 6: Accomplish at least 75 percent of all projects listed in the annual program.

Figure 7.2   IDOT quality objectives.

measure your success so you can share your story with the world? In order to define success for our organization, we tied our overall organization's quality objectives to critical outcomes that had been established in our strategic plan (see Figure 7.2).

This allowed us to meet the standard requirement in a manner that was familiar to our employees. With this exercise completed, we moved on to the more difficult task of translating these broad organizational objectives into more-specific quality objectives at relevant functions and levels within the organization.

TRANSLATING THE QUALITY OBJECTIVES

As mentioned in Chapter 5 of this book, middle managers have the most difficult job in the entire organization. Top management develops the strategy that will take the organization where it needs to go. In order for frontline employees to execute that strategy, the organization's middle management must find a way to translate the broad goals and targets of the executive strategy into specific, measurable objectives.

For example, reducing the number of fatalities on Illinois highways may be a worthwhile goal, but it doesn't mean much to a highway maintainer out in the field unless someone translates that overall objective into a specific measure that the maintainer can strive to attain. The highway maintainer may not understand exactly how to reduce the overall fatality rate, but she *does* understand what is needed to reduce the amount of time to convert a roadway from snow covered to wet (bare) pavement on the snow route that she drives. By reducing the time to wet pavement, the maintainer has improved the surface conditions of the roadway, which then makes travel through her section safer. This directly supports the overall goal of reducing fatalities on Illinois roadways.

In order to implement the strategy, the overall quality objectives must be cascaded to all levels and functions of the organization. In order to accomplish this task at IDOT, top management ordered the establishment of objectives and measures for all bureaus and sections within the quality management system. The new objectives and measures were communicated in a variety of ways: electronic collaboration sites, centralized bulletin boards, bureau, section, and personal scorecards, and through discussion in individual staff meetings at various levels within the organization.

What was important was not the methodology employed but the requirement that the objectives and measures directly support the achievement of the department's overall quality objectives and are effectively communicated and understood by employees.

I believe that personal scorecards are the best way to facilitate the communication and understanding needed to drive continual improvement of processes. The scorecard need not be complex but it should contain a balanced set of objectives and measures. In their best-selling book *The Strategy-Focused Organization*, Norton and Kaplan provide some excellent examples of personal scorecards that have been employed in successful organizations. Our scorecards are similar in structure and style. An example of one of our scorecards is available in Appendix A.

INTERNAL COMMUNICATION

Internal communication is often a difficult beast to tame in a large organization. This is because very few organizations manage communication as a process. Effective communication is a process just like every other activity in an organization and it must be managed with specific objectives and measures that define the terms of success. The ISO 9001 standard helped us identify the measurable objectives we needed to achieve:

Objective 1: Employees understand the importance of meeting customer as well as statutory requirements (clause 5.1a)

Objective 2: Employees understand the quality policy (clause 5.3d)

Objective 3: Employees understand their responsibilities and authorities (clause 5.5.1)

Objective 4: Employees understand the relevance and importance of their activities and how they contribute to the achievement of the organization's objectives (clause 6.2.2e)

With these four main objectives identified, it's not a difficult exercise to develop an effective communication plan. We simply made a concerted effort to determine the specific needs of our users (that is, the most effective means of communicating this information) and then planned the communication processes necessary to achieve the objectives. The most important component of the exercise was the establishment of a process to continually measure and improve the communication process. We mapped out a process based on the plan–do–check–act methodology. See Figure 7.3.

As noted in Figure 7.3, the two major measures of effectiveness are the annual employee survey and our internal audit program. Several specific questions were created for the annual employee survey to assess overall employee understanding. Responses to these questions provide a broad

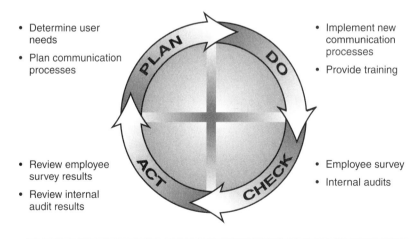

Figure 7.3 PDCA for the overall quality management system.

overview of the effectiveness of our communication processes. While the results are a lagging measure, they allow us to identify trends and determine appropriate goals for the next planning cycle.

Our internal audit team performs a more focused assessment of our organization's internal communication processes during annual internal audits. Our auditors not only review processes and documentation, they are trained to actively engage the auditee in a discussion. Their primary objective is to determine the level of conformance to the requirements of the ISO 9001 standard and documented procedures, and we believe that mandate includes the objectives outlined in the preceding section.

One of the simplest ways for our auditors to determine the effectiveness of our communication processes is to simply ask employees, "In your own words, what does the quality policy mean to you?" Our auditors often use this question to quickly assess the effectiveness of internal communication in specific areas. If the employee demonstrates an adequate understanding of the quality policy, they usually also understand the importance of meeting requirements and how their activities contribute to the success of the organization. If the employee fumbles with the answer to this question or simply answers, "I don't know," the auditor must dig deeper to determine the level of conformance and identify potential problems.

Measuring the effectiveness of internal communication processes isn't always a pleasant exercise. The results of employee surveys and internal audits can often be downright discouraging for management, but unless the effort is made to assess the current situation, there can be no hope for improvement. History abounds with examples of the need to quantify the situation at hand with facts and data in order to make effective decisions. In his Pulitzer Prize–winning book *1776*, David McCullough reveals that during George Washington's first month as commander of the Continental Army, he requested a report on the army's supply of gunpowder. The report determined there was barely enough powder for nine rounds per man. McCullough writes that Washington was so stunned by the report, he could not speak for a half hour. Washington eventually recovered from his bout of aphonia and worked diligently to procure the necessary armaments to bring the Continental Army to a respectable level of fighting strength. Had Washington not chosen to face the brutal truth and assess the current situation, the world might be a much different place.

It takes real moral courage to be a leader. Only those individuals who are willing to ask the question, "What am I not doing well?" can ever hope to become a great leader. For this reason, we provide an opportunity for our employees to share their thoughts with management anonymously. In 2007 alone, we received over 500 comments. To say that a few of the comments were negative might be a bit of an understatement, but we quickly discovered there was gold laced within the lattice of this raw ore. It simply needed to be mined.

Once we have the results of the annual employee survey and our internal audits in hand, we analyze the information during our required management reviews with the goal of identifying opportunities for improvement. The outputs of these reviews are typically revisions to our communication processes, which are tied to specific, measurable outcomes. Revisions are made to our internal communication processes, and the cycle begins again.

Over the course of the past few years, we've taken our share of hard knocks. We've missed opportunities, we've mishandled many issues, and we've often missed the mark with our message. It's been difficult, but we've learned a lot about our organization and the importance of communication. Most importantly, we've learned that the most critical part of effective communication is to simply start an honest dialogue with our employees. If there is one piece of advice I can share with managers who wish to improve their internal communication processes it is this: *get out of your office and talk to your people.* You don't have to be eloquent, you don't have to be inspirational—you just need to talk. Give them information; listen to their concerns; ask them for their suggestions. The absolutely worst action you can take is no action. Nothing is more important in an organization than communication, and nothing is more detrimental to morale than silence. Get out of your office and communicate with your employees.

MANAGEMENT REPRESENTATIVE

In our organization, many past improvement initiatives have been assigned to middle managers, with predictably unspectacular results. Managers at lower levels simply do not possess the authority or emotional capital necessary to enforce change at an organizational level. The ISO 9001 standard recognizes the importance of this issue and requires that top management of the organization appoint one of their own (a member of management) to champion the quality management system. The standard has some specific requirements for this individual, which include:

- Ensuring that processes needed for the QMS are established, implemented, and maintained

- Reporting to top management on the performance of the QMS

- Ensuring the promotion of awareness of customer requirements throughout the organization

It's extremely important that management chooses this individual carefully. In identifying a management representative, top management should consider the recommended competencies listed in Table 7.1.

At IDOT, the secretary appointed John Webber, assistant to the secretary for strategic planning, as the ISO management representative. John had served as a champion for many past improvement initiatives and had the track record, the skills, and the authority required to keep the certification program on track. John had the perfect leadership style for the position because he believed that anyone in the organization could be a leader, regardless of their title. When looking to assign responsibility for a specific initiative related to the ISO 9001 certification program, John looked for the individual with the best skills to lead the effort. He was focused on results, not status. The secretary of transportation gave John broad authority to select any employee at any time to fill a role in an improvement initiative. By choosing employees who displayed the proper mix of skills needed for the success of important initiatives without regard to status or rank, John uncovered real leadership within obscure areas of the organization. Many of the employees John selected to lead change teams have gone on to fill critical needs within other areas of the Department. Without John's instincts for finding leaders in unlikely places, these employees would never have risen to management levels within the organization.

As time passed and the management system began to grow, the demands on John's time also grew. Though John had done an excellent job of assembling teams to handle the various improvement initiatives, there remained a great deal of work simply to coordinate and manage this movement. John's primary responsibility as the management representative was

Table 7.1 Management representative competencies.

Knowledge	Skills	Attributes
Organizational strategy	Communication	Enthusiastic
Quality management	Mentoring and coaching	Diplomatic
Organizational capabilities	Facilitation	Empathetic
Executive staff capabilities	Strategic planning	Decisive leader
Political dynamics	Problem solving	Inspirational
Business administration	Conflict resolution	Respected

to champion the ISO 9001 certification program and promote the awareness of customer requirements throughout the organization. Unfortunately, John found himself tied to the computer and the phone most days as he worked long hours keeping people connected and improvement initiatives moving forward, reviewing and revising quality policies, and coordinating audits and corrective actions.

John is a natural consensus builder and a visionary. He is most effective when he can engage management and employees in a discussion and secure their support for improvement initiatives. Unfortunately, John was unable use these strengths to move the program into all areas of the Department because he was tied up with the tremendous effort needed to coordinate this large of a program. A new approach was needed. That's when my phone rang.

John asked me to stop by his office to discuss the future of the certification program. He explained to me that someone was needed to take over day-to-day oversight of the certification program. John and other members of management believed that my experience and skills would be a good match for this type of position. It didn't take much convincing to secure my agreement. I knew that coordinating the ISO 9001 effort would be a tremendous learning opportunity for me and would provide me the opportunity to become a change agent in an organization that was committed to improvement. I quickly accepted the position, and John and I began immediately to collaborate to determine the most effective division of responsibilities and authorities.

What emerged from this collaboration was very much a team-oriented approach. As the management representative, John is the large offensive lineman who blocks and creates the opening. As the ISO coordinator, it's my job to carry the ball. Using the results of measures, management reviews, and audit results, it's my responsibility to identify opportunities for improvement and to develop implementation plans. John is responsible for securing the commitment of management in affected areas and ensuring the availability of resources necessary for our improvement initiatives. This division of responsibilities has allowed both of us to focus our efforts on the things we do best, and has improved the success of our improvement initiatives.

Leadership is critical to the success of an ISO 9001 certification program. The standard defines important objectives for top management to achieve in order to demonstrate their commitment and lead the organization effectively. A concentrated focus on the achievement of these objectives will produce the vision and resolve necessary to push an ordinary organization toward world-class performance.

SUMMARY

- Effective leadership in any organization requires a mixture of clear vision and stern resolve.

- It's extremely important to build management commitment into a management system.

- The implementation of the ISO 9001 standard is most effective when it is tied directly to the organization's strategic plan.

- The quality policy defines what quality means for the entire organization. Don't explain ISO 9001 to your employees—explain the quality policy to them. Whenever practicable, work it into every presentation, every meeting, every conversation.

- Translate your quality policy and your quality objectives into something each employee can strive to achieve.

- Communication is a process just like every other activity in your organization. Set measurable objectives for communication processes and continually evaluate your progress.

- Only those who are willing to ask the question, "What am I not doing well?" can ever hope to become a great leader.

- Get out and talk to your people! Nothing is more important to an organization than communication, and nothing is more detrimental to morale and motivation than silence.

- The choice of management representative is a critical component of a successful certification program. Choose a member of top management who has the skills, knowledge, and attributes to truly champion the cause to all employees.

8

Involvement of People

Individual commitment to a group effort—that is what makes a team work, a company work, a society work, a civilization work.

—Vince Lombardi

INTRODUCTION

In 2009 the Pittsburgh Steelers steamrolled the competition through the playoffs and then beat the Arizona Cardinals in the Super Bowl to earn their sixth Super Bowl win. One of the hallmarks of a great team is that everyone on the team is focused on achieving a common goal and each member knows exactly what he must do to help the team achieve that goal. For the Pittsburgh Steelers last season, the common goal was winning the Super Bowl. For 16 grueling weeks each player concentrated on doing his job with the goal of helping the team accomplish its objective. The running backs understood that they needed to establish the Steelers' running game so the opposition's defense would open up enough for quarterback Ben Roethlisberger to use the team's talented wide receivers. The defensive line understood that they needed to pressure the opposition's quarterback in order to force turnovers that the offense could then convert into points. During one of the playoff games, I remember a football analyst saying of the Pittsburgh Steelers, "Every man on that field knows what he needs to do to allow the team to win." What the analyst said of the Pittsburgh Steelers is true of any successful team.

The purpose of an organization is to multiply the contributions of each individual so that the sum is greater than the individual parts. In order to achieve its full potential, an organization must have employees who are fully involved. The 2009 Super Bowl was not won by the Steelers' head coach

Mike Tomlin, nor was it won by the team's star linebacker, James Harrison. It was won by a team of fully involved individuals. Each team member executed his responsibilities to the extent of his abilities. The team's commitment to the singular goal of winning the Super Bowl energized each player in a profound manner and allowed each team member to use his unique talents to help the team reach its goal. Great organizations follow the same concept with just two small differences: the chances of injury are greatly diminished and 100 million people are rarely watching their performance.

OBJECTIVES AND EXPECTATIONS

It seems that one can not read a business magazine these days without finding at least one article or column stressing the need for innovation in the new business environment. Many business experts claim the pace of change is so fast today that only companies who can continually innovate at a rapid pace will be able to survive and prosper. As a result, many executives and managers believe that setting rigid boundaries and expectations for their employees will stifle innovation and creativity. I can certainly agree that micromanaging employees will create an atmosphere that is not conducive to creativity, but I disagree with the premise that the establishment of boundaries and expectations will stifle creativity.

One of the greatest achievements in western society was the development of the chromatic scale during the European Renaissance. The chromatic scale is a method of dividing up an octave by using the twelfth root of two. An octave is an interval between two notes—the higher note being twice the frequency of the lower note. The chromatic scale divides the octave into twelve tones. These tones are the basis for the black and white keys of the piano. Think about that for just a second—musicians took all of the possible frequencies available and reduced them down to a manageable few (the modern piano has just 88 keys). By creating such strict boundaries and standards, wouldn't this stifle creativity and innovation? There were certainly detractors who believed so, and they were quite vocal at times. Incredibly enough, the opposite happened. Musical creativity exploded in the next few centuries, resulting in a kaleidoscopic range of musical diversity from J. S. Bach to Metallica. By standardizing music, composers didn't stifle innovation—they *enabled* it. Regardless of whether they are creating a symphony or a spreadsheet, people need clear boundaries and expectations in order to perform at a high level.

QUALITY POLICY
AND QUALITY OBJECTIVES

In Chapter 7, we discussed the importance of the quality policy (clause 5.3) and quality objectives (clause 5.4.1) in demonstrating leadership and effective management. The quality policy and quality objectives are also critical elements in securing employee involvement. W. Edwards Deming believed that constancy of purpose was critical for the ultimate success of an organization and that the efforts of all employees should be focused on improving quality. Constancy of purpose toward ever-improving quality is the backbone of Deming's management philosophy, and he believed it was essential that management create a written statement that explains the aims and purposes of the company and that they continually provide evidence of commitment to the fulfillment of this statement. Given Deming's tremendous influence in the field of quality management, it should come as no surprise that ISO/TC 176 would include a requirement that management create documented statements of a quality policy and quality objectives.

As discussed in Chapter 7, the quality policy and quality objectives define the goals and objectives of a management system into something employees can work to achieve. When properly structured and communicated, they can galvanize your organization in the same manner that the goal of winning the Super Bowl can galvanize an NFL team. The involvement of employees will improve when they understand how their activities can support the achievement of the organization's quality policy and quality objectives. Communication of the quality policy and the quality objectives should take place as often as possible using a wide variety of means such as presentations, staff meetings, bulletin boards, and mailings.

CLAUSE 5.5.1: RESPONSIBILITIES
AND AUTHORITIES

Clause 5.5.1 requires that top management ensure that responsibilities and authorities are defined and communicated within the organization. At the Illinois Department of Transportation, we addressed this requirement in three ways: through the use of job descriptions, organizational charts, and documented procedures. During our internal audits, we generally began by meeting with the manager of the area we were auditing. We would often ask the manager how responsibilities and authorities were communicated within the office. The manager would proudly display a colorful and descriptive organizational chart. After we left the office of the manager, we would ask each person we interviewed if they had a copy of an organizational chart. Nine times out of ten, they couldn't find one or they had an old organizational chart that did not match the colorful organizational chart that the manager showed us. It wasn't that the manager wasn't trying to keep this documentation current, and it certainly wasn't the fault of the employees. The system just couldn't keep up with the pace of change.

In my opinion, organizational charts and job descriptions are fine but they are a bit too restrictive for the 21st century. Organizations need to be more nimble and flexible in the new business environment, and these types of devices are holdovers from the old business environment of the 20th century, which was far more static. This is one area of the ISO 9001 standard where an organization should rethink the way it approaches this requirement. The use of appropriate technology can go a long way toward improving the communication of responsibilities and authorities throughout the entire organization. Concepts like wikis and personal/collaborative Web pages (Microsoft SharePoint, Oracle Collaboration Suite, IBM Lotus Notes, and so on) are great ways to define and document responsibilities and authorities.

CLAUSE 6.2.2: COMPETENCE, TRAINING, AND AWARENESS

The requirements of clause 6.2.2 are often confusing to many people. I've never understood this confusion, as the concepts are rather basic to effective management. In order for an organization to be successful, it needs employees with specific skill sets. Accountants need to understand how to conduct double-entry bookkeeping, chefs need to understand how to cook a dinner, and delivery personnel need to understand how to operate a vehicle. When hiring new people or establishing new positions, the organization needs to determine the minimum competencies required for each position— what skills are required, what training is necessary, how much experience is essential. When gaps exist between the competency requirements and the actual skills, training, and experience of an employee, the organization must provide training or take other actions to satisfy these needs. Once action has been taken, the organization must evaluate the effectiveness of those actions in developing the necessary competencies. Records of education, training, skills, and experience are required to be maintained. Most importantly, all employees must understand the relevance and importance of their activities and how they contribute to the achievement of the organization's objectives.

At IDOT, we have a bureau of personnel management that develops policies for the hiring, retention, and evaluation of all employees. Competencies are documented in job descriptions. When positions are vacated, interviews are conducted to identify candidates with the necessary skills, education, and training to best complete the responsibilities of the position. Competency gaps are identified during annual performance evaluations, and training is provided or other actions are taken as appropriate. Most training conducted includes an evaluation of the training's effectiveness through the administration of a written test or similar means. In any instances where the training provided does not include an evaluation of effectiveness, the employee's supervisor verifies the effectiveness of the actions taken.

DOES EVERYONE IN MY ORGANIZATION NEED TO BE AN ISO EXPERT?

Everyone in the organization does not need to be an ISO expert but they must understand the basic requirements of your quality management system. Some of the more important elements that must be understood by employees include:

- What to do when products/services do not conform to requirements

- How their activities contribute to the achievement of the organization's quality policy and quality objectives

- Which documents are needed for their job responsibilities, where to locate those documents, and how to ensure they are using the most current versions of those documents

- What records must be kept for their activities, how long these records must be kept, and where these records must be stored

Chapter 14 provides a sample training plan for ensuring that the appropriate competencies are developed in your organization.

HOW CAN I GET MY EMPLOYEES COMMITTED TO OUR ISO 9001 CERTIFICATION EFFORT?

Communication is consistently rated as one of the most important elements of effective management by employees and executives alike. Given the relative importance of communication it is surprising that executives spend so little of their time planning *how* they will communicate with their employees. I've often observed excellent planning and execution of many elements of a change initiative right up to the part when communication enters the picture; at that point, many executives believe they should just "wing it" and figure it out as they go along. This is a common and deadly mistake. Winning employee acceptance of an ISO 9001 certification effort requires careful planning and skillful execution. Chapter 14 provides an example of a communication plan to keep employees informed on the progress of the ISO 9001 certification program.

If you want employees to accept the precept that quality, customer satisfaction, and continual improvement are truly important, then you must lead the way. All of the new systems and requirements that are created to support the ISO 9001 certification effort must be embraced by management. If you desire your employees to use the organization's corrective action system, you must ensure that they see *you* use it as much as possible. If you want your employees to standardize and control their procedures, you must ensure that they see *you* embracing the same concepts whenever possible.

Trust happens when values and behavior match up. Employees will become involved and committed when they see that *you* are involved and committed.

SUMMARY

- In order to be successful, organizations must have employees who are fully involved in helping the team achieve its goal.

- In order to be involved, employees must have a common goal and a clear understanding of their responsibilities and how their activities contribute to the achievement of the organization's goals.

- The quality policy and quality objectives provide common goals for all employees to strive to achieve.

- The quality policy and quality objectives should be communicated to employees as often as possible.

- Common means that many organizations use to define and communicate responsibilities and authorities are job descriptions, organizational charts, and documented procedures.

- Organizations must determine minimum competencies for personnel performing work affecting requirements. When gaps exist between the competency requirements and the actual skills, training, and experience of an employee, the organization must provide training or take other actions to satisfy these needs.

- All employees do not need ISO 9001 training; they need training on the requirements of the organization's quality management system.

- Winning employee acceptance of an ISO 9001 certification effort requires careful planning and skillful execution.

- Employees will become involved and committed when they see that top management is involved and committed.

9

Process Approach

"Men's courses will foreshadow certain ends, to which,
if persevered in, they must lead," said Scrooge. "But if
the courses be departed from, the ends will change.

Say it is thus with what you show me!"

—Charles Dickens, *A Christmas Carol*

INTRODUCTION

During his visit with the ghost of Christmas future, Ebenezer Scrooge quickly developed a greater understanding of the relationship between means and ends. The means by which Scrooge was living his life day by day were hurtling him toward a predictable destiny of despair and doom. By seeing the tragic end to which his current course was leading him, Ebenezer Scrooge was able to change the means by which he lived his life. By changing the means, he changed the end result.

An understanding of the relationship between means and ends is one of the foundations of the philosophy of quality management. Albert Einstein is reported to have once defined insanity as "doing the same thing over and over again and expecting a different result." I can find no conclusive evidence to support that Einstein ever uttered this phrase, but the truth of the statement is definitely not in question. Many organizations struggle through operations on a daily basis with managers exhorting their employees to do more with less by setting quotas and insisting on improved performance from each employee. Though well-intentioned, these leaders lack an understanding that the means they demand their employees follow will invariably lead them to the same ends time and time again regardless of quotas, demands, pleading, or exhortations. These managers would be wise to learn from the example of Ebenezer Scrooge: if one wishes to achieve different ends they must first change the means. In the field of quality management, we refer to ends as *outputs* and means as *processes.*

WHAT IS A PROCESS?

When I was a kid, my grandmother would make pancakes every Saturday morning. I can remember marveling as this 95-pound woman wrestled a 20-pound grill onto the top of her stove. After greasing down the grill, she'd move on to the task of creating those wonderful, fluffy pancakes. First she sifted the flour, baking powder, and salt together. Then she stirred in buttermilk and real butter. Finally, she added some eggs and lightly whipped the batter exactly twenty times. Every batch of pancakes was absolutely superb—smooth velvety bites of heaven. How was my grandmother able to make such delicious pancakes? The answer is simple—she used a recipe. On a piece of paper she had written exact measurements for all of the necessary ingredients and step-by-step procedures regarding how they should be combined. By following this recipe each and every Saturday morning, Grandma could be assured her pancakes would turn out exactly the same every time she made them.

A process is very similar to a recipe. It is a set of interrelated or interacting activities that transforms inputs into outputs. In the case of Grandma's pancake recipe, the inputs are the raw ingredients (flour, salt, buttermilk, eggs), the equipment (stove, grill, mixing bowls), and the expertise (Grandma wasn't born a pancake expert—she had to learn how to do it just like anyone else). The activities are the various steps in the recipe—mixing, sifting, cooking, and flipping. In order to achieve a predictable result in either the kitchen or the office, we must follow our "recipe" (process) faithfully each and every time.

An organization is a lot like my grandma's kitchen; there are a lot of different outputs to be produced and a lot of different processes (recipes) that need to be completed. Some of the processes within your organization are simple and probably don't need to be documented. My grandma's fried chicken recipe was simple: eggs, flour, salt, and oil. She never wrote it down because she felt it wasn't necessary. Grandma could easily replicate her fried chicken recipe from memory. It is likely there are other processes within your organization that are more complex or are not completed very often and probably should be documented in a procedure. Every Thanksgiving my grandma made squash pie. The recipe for squash pie was considerably more complex than her fried chicken recipe, and grandma only made it once a year. To ensure that Uncle George wasn't disappointed when he bit into a slice of her squash pie, Grandma kept a written recipe and followed it each year when she made her masterpiece.

The ISO 9001 standard requires an organization to adopt a process approach to the management of its activities and resources. By managing activities and related resources as a process, an organization can achieve better and more consistent results.

POLICIES, PROCESSES, AND PROCEDURES

Most organizations have a dizzying array of policies, processes, and procedures. It's important to develop a common understanding of the meaning of each of these terms in the context of the ISO 9001 standard. A *policy* communicates the overall intentions and direction of an organization. In other words, it tells us what we do and why we do it. A *process* communicates what activities are needed and the order in which they need to be completed. A *procedure* is a specific way to carry out an activity or a part of a process. See Figure 9.1.

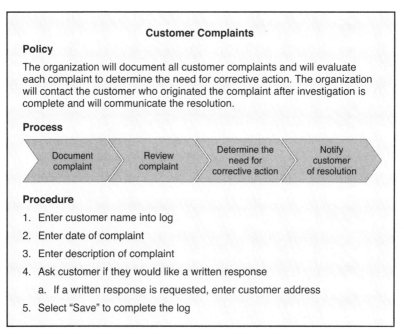

Figure 9.1 Examples of a policy, process, and procedure.

A clear understanding of the differences between a policy, a process, and a procedure is important to the correct interpretation and application of the ISO 9001 standard requirements in your organization.

CLAUSE 4.1: GENERAL REQUIREMENTS

Clause 4.1 requires the organization to identify the processes needed for the quality management system and to determine the sequence and interaction of those processes. Processes that are outsourced must be identified in the quality management system along with the method of control used to ensure conformity with requirements. Identifying processes in an established public-sector organization can be extremely difficult. Many public-sector organizations provide a multifarious collection of products and services and therefore are required to execute thousands of activities during the course of a year. With so many activities going on at once it's easy to get lost in the complexity of operations. If you find yourself in this situation, it is suggested you begin by taking an inventory of all of the activities performed in the organization. This can be accomplished in a number of ways: by an audit, by brainstorming sessions, or by the use of turtle diagrams. Turtle diagrams are a quick and easy way to document the specifics of a process. They are named *turtle* diagrams because of the way they resemble the body of a turtle. The process is the "shell" and the inputs and outputs are the "head" and "tail." The process objectives/measures, competency requirements, related resources, and controls are the "feet." See Figure 9.2.

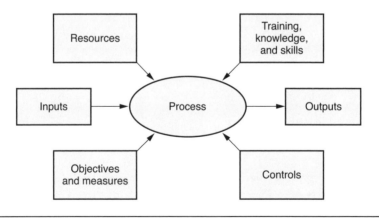

Figure 9.2   Turtle diagram.

Turtle diagrams are great tool for quickly documenting important information about a process and the way it interrelates with other processes within an organization. Once turtle diagrams are completed for all processes, it is simply a matter of finding a large, blank wall and taping the turtle diagrams up one by one, concentrating on matching the output of one process with the input of another. By conducting this exercise, one can quickly identify how work flows through the most complex of organizations.

At the Illinois Department of Transportation, we started by identifying our core processes (see Figure 9.3). The core processes are the high-level processes that directly translate the needs of the traveling public into the built facility.

Next, we identified the key processes within each core process, as shown in Figure 9.4. The intent was to identify the larger, cross-functional processes that have a high impact on the traveling public and overall project quality. The key processes are the individual activities that must be completed for the successful execution of each core process.

Once the key processes were identified, we then determined the support processes necessary to support the accomplishment of quality objectives, conformance with project requirements, and continual improvement

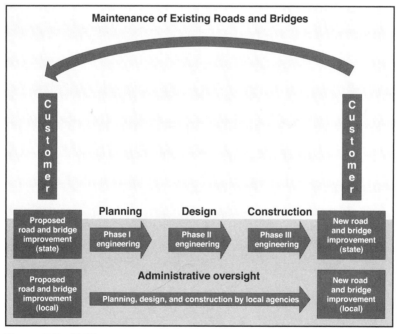

Figure 9.3 IDOT core processes.

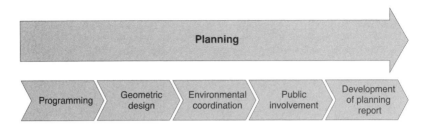

Figure 9.4   The key processes that comprise the IDOT core process of planning.

of the core processes. Figure 9.5 shows the major support processes as inputs into the core processes. These inputs are the major resources necessary to implement the Department's core processes and to accomplish its primary mission.

Once all of our processes and their interrelations were documented, we tackled section 7.0 of the standard. Section 7.0 contains requirements for product realization. This section can be extremely confusing for a service organization, as many of the terms utilized appear at first blush to apply only to manufacturing organizations. It's important to understand that these requirements are included to control the realization processes that the organization has developed to create products and services that meet customer requirements. The following pages provide IDOT's interpretation of how the requirements of sections 7.1, 7.3, 7.5, and 7.6 can be applied to a service organization. Section 7.2 is explained in Chapter 6 and section 7.4 is explained in Chapter 13.

CLAUSE 7.1: PLANNING OF PRODUCT/SERVICE REALIZATION

Clause 7.1 requires the organization to plan and develop the processes needed for product realization. The output of this planning must be in a form that is suitable for the organization's method of operations. At IDOT, quality planning is achieved through the development and implementation of policies and procedures that define the controls needed to implement the core processes of planning, design, and construction of road and bridge improvements. The outputs of IDOT's quality planning are fully documented policies and procedures that form part of the overall

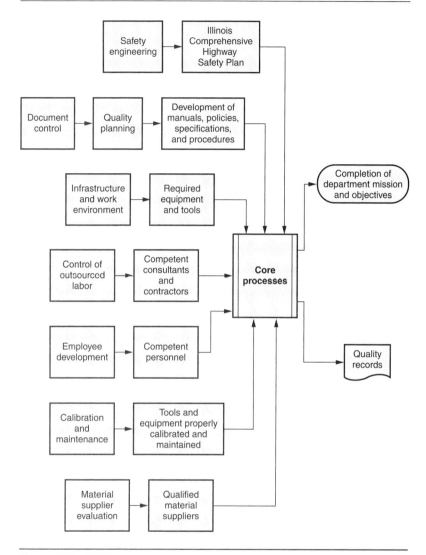

Figure 9.5 IDOT support processes.

quality management system. These documents include operational manuals, departmental orders and policies, standard contract specifications, and work instructions. In order to ensure conformance to the requirements of the ISO 9001 standard, we required that each document be reviewed against the requirements of the standard.

CLAUSE 7.3.1: DESIGN AND DEVELOPMENT PLANNING

Design and development planning concerns any design activities your organization utilizes in the development of products and services. Clause 7.3.1 requires that planning be conducted to determine the necessary controls required to effectively manage the interfaces between different groups involved in design and development to ensure effective communication and clear assignment of responsibility. At IDOT, we already had design manuals and policy memoranda that documented the processes and procedures governing the design of roads and bridges. We initiated a review of these documents to ensure that all of the ISO 9001 standard requirements for design and development were adequately addressed.

CLAUSE 7.3.2: DESIGN AND DEVELOPMENT INPUTS

Design and development inputs include important information regarding the requirements of the product/service that is being designed. These inputs must be reviewed for adequacy to ensure that all requirements are complete, unambiguous, and not in conflict with each other. At IDOT, the major input into the core process of design was the output of our planning process: a report that documented all of the requirements for each road and bridge improvement. Other inputs included established highway standard plans and standard specifications for road and bridge construction. This information was derived from previous designs of road and bridge components that were successful and cost-effective.

CLAUSE 7.3.3: DESIGN AND DEVELOPMENT OUTPUTS

Design and development outputs must provide appropriate information for purchasing and production/service realization. They must be provided in a form that allows verification against the design and development inputs and must be approved prior to release. The major outputs of the IDOT design process are approved plans, specifications, and estimates that contain or reference all the information necessary for the construction of a specific road and/or bridge improvement. These documents are reviewed for adequacy and approved before use.

CLAUSE 7.3.4: DESIGN AND DEVELOPMENT REVIEW

Reviews of design and development are required to be performed in accordance with planned arrangements. Participants in design and development reviews must include representatives of functions concerned with the design and development stage being reviewed. Within IDOT, formal design reviews are required at the preliminary development stage (roughly 60 percent complete) and also the pre-final development stage (95 percent complete) for most projects. More complex projects may require more frequent reviews. The preliminary design review is a group meeting that involves a thorough review and discussion of the preliminary plans with representatives of functions concerned with the design stage being reviewed. The pre-final review is an individual review of the final plans and specifications that is conducted by several areas of IDOT in tandem to ensure that all comments from the preliminary plan review were addressed in a satisfactory manner and that the plans and specifications meet all of IDOT's requirements.

CLAUSE 7.3.5: DESIGN AND DEVELOPMENT VERIFICATION

Once the pre-final design review is complete, a formal review must be conducted of the design output (plans, specifications, and estimates) against the design inputs (project report) to ensure that all requirements have been addressed. At IDOT, the plans, specifications, and estimates are reviewed against the requirements of the project report to ensure that all requirements have been satisfied by the design. This verification is documented by the completion of a form that is maintained in the project files.

CLAUSE 7.3.6: DESIGN AND DEVELOPMENT VALIDATION

Validation is confirmation through the provision of objective evidence that the requirements for a specific intended use or application have been fulfilled. Roads and bridges are extremely costly to build. It would be extremely unfortunate for us to discover after expending several million dollars that a particular design for a bridge is not sufficient to handle the anticipated traffic load. In order to ensure that this does not occur, it is important for us to validate the ability of the bridge design to withstand the load for which it was designed. This is possible through a number of different ways. Simple road and bridge designs are validated through adherence to specified design policies. These types of improvements have been validated through previous designs that have been constructed and evaluated to ensure that the constructed improvement is capable of meeting the requirements for the specified application. Improvements involving new roadways and structures often require validation through detailed engineering analysis and complex mathematical calculations. Structural analysis is performed on proposed bridge designs, hydraulic analysis is used to validate the proposed capacity of drainage structures, and pavement designs are validated by the use of engineering analysis and design calculations. The objective evidence supporting the validation process is the records of the necessary calculations and analysis.

CLAUSE 7.3.7: CONTROL OF DESIGN AND DEVELOPMENT CHANGES

At IDOT, changes to the design plans and specifications are occasionally required during the construction phase. Roads and bridges are large public works projects, and it is nearly impossible to anticipate every contingency during the design process. Unknown utility conflicts, unforeseen subsurface conditions, and availability of materials may require a change to the design of the project, and a contract change order is initiated. Contract change orders are implemented through a process that ensures design changes are necessary, germane to the intent of the contract, and properly approved by a relevant authority.

CLAUSE 7.5.1: CONTROL OF PRODUCTION AND SERVICE PROVISION

In order to achieve consistent results, production of products and implementation of services must be controlled through the use of suitable equipment, availability of product/service requirements, appropriate monitoring and measurement methods, and adequate procedures for the release of the product/service and all required delivery and post-delivery activities. At IDOT, road and bridge construction activities are controlled through the use of the Standard Specifications for Road and Bridge Construction. This document is published by IDOT and contains procedures and specifications necessary to ensure that minimum requirements are met and that production is completed under controlled conditions.

CLAUSE 7.5.2: VALIDATION OF PROCESSES FOR PRODUCTION AND SERVICE PROVISION

Validation of all production and service realization processes where the resulting output can not be verified by subsequent monitoring or measurement is required by the ISO 9001 standard. Validation provides objective evidence that the output of the process meets requirements. Records of validation are required to be maintained. A good example of a validation activity at IDOT occurred when we made a major improvement to our corrective and preventive action (CAPA) system. For the first three years of our certification, we had used a paper-based system. In early 2009, we developed an electronic system to initiate, track, and verify all corrective and preventive actions. Since there was no way to verify the adequacy of the system by monitoring or measuring, we needed to validate the new process. Before any work was initiated to design the new system, we completed a vigorous analysis of requirements for an electronic CAPA system. Once the system was completed, we formed a focus group of employees who were representative of the diverse nature of our organization. Different trials were designed to test the system in such a manner that an analysis of the ability of the system to satisfy all requirements could be made at the conclusion of the validation period. Several areas of improvement were noted when the validation exercise was concluded, and the CAPA system was revised to address the problem areas. The CAPA system was then revalidated by a similar exercise. The second validation exercise produced zero defects, so the system was rolled out to the entire organization. Records of both validation exercises were maintained in accordance with the requirements of the IDOT quality manual.

CLAUSE 7.5.3: IDENTIFICATION AND TRACEABILITY

All products and services are required to be adequately identified during production/implementation to ensure traceability. At IDOT, projects are identified by the use of contract numbers and state job authorization numbers. These numbers provide the traceability necessary to conduct effective audits and for proper investigation of corrective action.

CLAUSE 7.5.4: CUSTOMER PROPERTY

This clause really had us stumped at IDOT. The ISO 9001 standard requires organizations to exercise care with customer property while it is under the organization's control. How can this clause possibly apply to a state department of transportation? All of the property, equipment, and material used in a construction project are owned by the state of Illinois. It seemed so foreign to us that we even excluded this clause from our initial certification. It wasn't until a few months later, when we started looking at the bigger picture, that we figured it out. While it is true that a road, bridge, or public right-of-way within the limits of a project is owned by the state of Illinois and therefore, by extension, IDOT, there are still many instances where this clause applies to our work. Many construction projects involve public utilities that could be damaged by construction activity, and, therefore, care must be exercised by IDOT to ensure that these utilities are not damaged. Similarly, road and bridge construction improvements often can result in the discharge of pollutants such as sediment, diesel fuel, and construction materials (cement and concrete) into public waterways. Once again, care must be exercised by IDOT to minimize the impacts of these pollutants to public waterways. Through a deeper understanding of the intent of the standard, we were able to address this requirement in a way that enhanced our operations.

CLAUSE 7.5.5: PRESERVATION OF PRODUCT

The ISO 9001 standard requires that the organization preserve the conformity of products or services during internal processing. This includes the constituent parts of a product. At IDOT, this can range from ensuring that aggregate stored on a construction job site is properly segregated to prevent contamination with other materials to maintaining effective traffic control to prevent traffic from traveling on new concrete patches until the patch has cured and a sufficient level of strength has been achieved.

CLAUSE 7.6: CONTROL OF MONITORING AND MEASUREMENT EQUIPMENT

Proper monitoring and measurement of products and services is essential to ensure that requirements have been achieved. In order to ensure that measurement and monitoring undertaken is accurate, the equipment and devices used to measure and monitor must be calibrated at appropriate intervals. The ISO 9001 standard requires calibration to be conducted according to measurement standards traceable to international or national measurement standards. In instances where international or national standards do not exist, the organization must document the basis of calibration. In addition, the standard requires that monitoring and measurement equipment be properly maintained and safeguarded against adjustments that would invalidate the measurement result. All monitoring and measurement equipment must be clearly identified to enable its calibration status to be determined. At IDOT, most of our monitoring and measurement equipment is calibrated to ASTM standards, and the calibration status is identified by stickers that display the date the equipment was last calibrated and the date of the next required calibration. Procedures to ensure that monitoring and measurement equipment is properly maintained and protected are clearly identified in appropriate documentation.

WHAT IS DOCUMENT CONTROL?

Of all the requirements of the ISO 9001 standard, I believe the document control requirement has caused the most confusion and apprehension at IDOT. Clause 4.2.3 requires the organization to control all documents required by the quality management system. What does document control mean in the context of the ISO 9001 standard? Document control means that each employee has easy access to the most current and appropriately approved versions of the documents needed to complete their responsibilities. It really is as simple as that. Effective implementation of this requirement is a little more difficult. God, as they say, is in the details.

In order to ensure that employees can access the most current versions of the documents needed to do their job, there needs to be some sort of distribution system. Regardless of whether the documents are electronic or paper-based, the organization must develop some way to get these documents into the hands of the employee for their use in implementing their activities. Furthermore, there needs to be some sort of identification applied to these documents in order for employees to differentiate one document from another and to ensure they are using the most current version. Finally, to ensure effective operations, these documents need to be properly reviewed for adequacy and approved prior to use. This applies not only to the original version but any later revisions to the document that may be necessary. These requirements apply to any external documents used by the organization as well. To ensure that adequate control is achieved, the ISO 9001 standard requires the organization to develop a documented procedure that defines the controls needed to meet all of the requirements of clause 4.2.3.

What documents must be controlled? Use this general rule: if your employees need a certain document to ensure the quality of their process and resulting outputs, the document needs to be controlled. At IDOT, we have several different methods of control for our many documents. Table 9.1 summarizes a few of the controls of our document control system.

Developing effective procedures for document control can seem overwhelming in a large organization. Remember that the concept is very simple. Many organizations overcomplicate the issue by requiring extreme standardization of all documents, which creates a behemoth of a document control system that bogs down the organization. Effective document control is simply a matter of getting the most current versions of quality documents into the hands of the employees who need them to complete their responsibilities. The minimum requirements of clause 4.2.3 of the ISO 9001 standard are more than sufficient to ensure effective control of documents. Create some simple procedures and controls that will enforce these requirements and don't worry about standardizing every single document. It's a nearly impossible task in a large organization and almost always a fruitless one.

WHY DO WE NEED TO RETAIN SO MANY RECORDS?

The ISO 9001 standard requires internal audits of the quality management system to ensure that the system conforms to planned arrangements and is effectively implemented and maintained. Audits can not be completed without a review of an organization's records, so the standard requires many records to be maintained to provide evidence of conformity to planned arrangements. To ensure that records are readily available for review, the standard requires the organization to develop a documented procedure that defines the controls needed for the identification, storage, protection, retrieval, retention time, and disposition of each record. IDOT controls its quality records through the use of retention schedules that are required by the State of Illinois Archive (Office of the Secretary of State). This was one area of the standard in which we were already meeting the requirement of the ISO 9001 standard. All that was required was for us to ensure that we were actually following our own established procedures. Table 9.2 contains several examples of IDOT records and the process used to maintain each record.

Table 9.1 Examples of controls for IDOT documents.

Document name	Unique identifier	Authority approval	Review interval	Current version identification	Archive	Availability
Quality manual	Title	ISO management representative	Annually	Date	Archived versions watermarked	Intranet
Departmental orders	Number and title	Secretary of transportation	Biannually	Date	Archived versions watermarked	Intranet
Departmental rules	Number and title	Joint Council on Administrative Rules	Minimum once every 5 years	Date	Archived versions watermarked	Intranet
Engineering plans	Contract number	Secretary of transportation	N/A	Date and signature	N/A	Hard copies controlled by district construction office
Forms	Number	Owner-recorded form creation/ modification form	Annually	Date	Archived version watermarked	Forms master list—intranet

Table 9.2   Examples of controls for IDOT records.

Record	Responsibility	Index	Filed	Retention period	Disposition
Management review meeting minutes	ISO management representative	Date of meeting	Room 300	Five years, then transfer to state records center for 10 years	Destroy after 15 years
Corrective and preventive actions	ISO quality assurance officer	Number	Room 334	Keep in room 334 for five years then transfer to state records center for 10 years	Destroy after 15 years
Internal audit records	Chief of audits	Date of audit	Room 125	Keep in room 125 for 10 years then transfer to state records center for 10 years	Destroy after 15 years
Engineering plans and contracts	Bureau of Design and Environment	Contract number	Room 330	Keep in room 330 for one year, then microfilm	Destroy originals. Maintain microfilm indefinitely.

The ISO 9001 standard requires a number of specific records to be maintained by the organization. To ensure complete understanding, the standard includes a reference to clause 4.2.4 in all areas of the standard where records are required to be maintained.

SUMMARY

- It is fruitless to continue doing things exactly the same each time and expecting a different result. If one wishes to change the ends, one must first change the means.

- A process is similar to a recipe. It is a set of interrelated or interacting activities that transforms inputs into outputs.

- A policy communicates what we do and why we do it. A process communicates what activities are needed and the order in which they need to be completed. A procedure communicates a specific way to conduct an activity or part of a process.

- Turtle diagrams are an easy way to quickly document the specifics of a process.

- Sections 7.1, 7.3, 7.5, and 7.6 of the ISO 9001 standard contain requirements for control of product/service realization processes.

- Document control means that each employee has easy access to the most current and appropriately approved version of the documents they need to complete their responsibilities.

- The ISO 9001 standard requires that records be maintained to demonstrate effective operation of the quality management system.

- Record control can be achieved by the use of simple matrices that document what records must be kept, how long they must be kept, who is responsible, where they are kept, and the ultimate disposition of the records.

10

System Approach to Management

*Every kingdom divided against itself is brought
to desolation; and every city or house divided against
itself shall not stand.*

—Matthew 12:25 (King James Version)

INTRODUCTION

"I want to go to McDonald's!!!" he shrieked. My girlfriend and I exchanged a look of dread as each of us shuddered involuntarily. We had been on our way to dinner at a nice restaurant when her four-year-old son had spotted the familiar golden arches. An intense negotiation session followed with the quality of the evening hanging in the balance. If my girlfriend was successful, we could look forward to a relaxing evening of quiet conversation and appetizing food. If her four-year-old outlasted her patience, it would be another hellish night filled with screaming children, grumpy parents, and unhealthy, mediocre food.

Don't get me wrong, I don't necessarily dislike McDonald's. It's an American institution after all—I just prefer to eat at a restaurant where the menu items are not perpetually draped in grease. The food really isn't very healthy nor does it taste particularly good to me but then again, McDonald's probably couldn't care less about my opinion. Their primary customers are children, and they do a phenomenal job of meeting their requirements (just ask my girlfriend's four-year-old son). In the midst of the worst economic climate since the Great Depression, McDonald's posted astounding annual results. Boasting over 30,000 restaurants in 119 countries, McDonald's serves an estimated 34 million customers a day. McDonald's franchises are highly sought-after business opportunities and they command a franchise fee of $45,000. The franchise fee is in addition to the capital necessary to pay for the equipment and workforce, which can cost more than a million dollars. If you wish to operate a McDonald's restaurant, you must pay the organization $45,000 before the first hamburger is served.

Why would anyone pay $45,000 for the right to make hamburgers? The answer, of course, is that franchisees are not purchasing a recipe for making hamburgers; they are purchasing a *system*—one of the greatest business systems ever devised, as a matter of fact. That system is really the magic behind the success of McDonald's. Pay close attention the next time you visit a McDonald's and marvel at the amazing organizational architecture that has evolved in the 69 years since Dick and Mac McDonald opened the first restaurant in San Bernardino, California. The McDonald brothers figured out a system for translating the needs of their customers into a product that met those needs in the cheapest, most efficient manner possible. I am no fan of the food, but the consistency of the product and the quality of the service are amazingly homogenous across the entire chain of restaurants. A Big Mac purchased in New York City is nearly identical to one purchased in Kansas City.

In the introduction of this book, we discussed how management systems provide the structure that allows organizations to shine. I can think of no better example in the business world than McDonald's—a business model that has managed to transform a single restaurant into a global economic powerhouse that generates nearly $70 billion in sales each year. McDonald's clearly understands the importance of a system approach to management.

McDonald's certainly has its detractors and has arguably skirted the area of corporate responsibility by serving food of mammoth proportions (the double Quarter Pounder value meal contains more than 1000 calories), but one must marvel at the incredible management system they have built. They have built a remarkable corporate culture with strong values and have managed to weave their organization into the very fabric of popular culture. When I speak to large audiences, I ask for a show of hands of how many can tell me the current McDonald's marketing slogan. Without fail, more than three-quarters of all in attendance raise their hands. Someone shouts out, "I'm lovin' it." I then ask everyone this question, "How many of you can tell me your organization's mission statement?" Ninety percent of the raised hands go down.

HOW CAN A SYSTEM APPROACH TO MANAGEMENT HELP US BETTER MANAGE OUR ORGANIZATION?

All work is a system of interrelated processes. The output of one process is most often an input into another process. Controlling the interrelation of these processes is critical to the success of any organization. By analyzing operations as a system, more effective decisions can be made regarding allocation of resources. A system approach also makes it easier to identify strategic improvements within the organization that can improve the ability of the core processes to meet the requirements of your customers and exceed their expectations. In this manner, a properly implemented management system is far superior to the typical productivity improvement initiatives that are launched in most organizations. Most improvement initiatives are launched by well-meaning executives with the intent of improving the organization's operations. Understanding that all work is a system of interrelated processes, let's take a look at an average improvement initiative and try to determine why it didn't work.

The director of a large government organization is not satisfied with the agency's current performance in the area of processing vendor contracts and decides to kick off an improvement initiative using the current flavor of the month—Six Sigma. The organization procures the services of a high-priced quality improvement consultant to provide training to each area involved in contract processing. Current operations and monthly processing capabilities look like Figure 10.1.

What is the output of this core process? Well, it can't be any more than 70 contracts per month, right? The current capability of bureau C is only 70 contracts per month, so the most contracts that can be processed in a given month by the core process is 70, regardless of how many contracts the other bureaus process. Six Sigma training is completed, and the manager of bureau B is really fired up. She works diligently with her staff for the next six months to complete some powerful improvements in her bureau that drastically reduce the amount of time needed by her staff to complete their responsibilities. As a result, employees in bureau B are now able to process 110 contracts per month! Not to be outdone, the manager of bureau E sees this improvement initiative as a way to get ahead in the organization. He rallies his troops to battle, and after seven months of long days and nights, his employees are able to reduce their processing time to new lows and now can process 110 contracts per month! An increase in productivity of 31 percent! The director is thrilled!

Meanwhile, the manager in bureau A has tried to secure the necessary funds to upgrade her equipment but was dismayed to find much of the

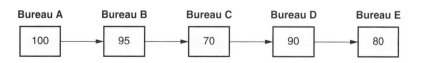

Figure 10.1 Example process capability.

operating budget unavailable to her. (The managers in bureau B and E were much more persuasive and therefore received the lion's share of available resources.) Her employees tried a few small changes but weren't really able to achieve much in the way of productivity increases. Bureau A's productivity remained at 100 contracts per month.

The manager in bureau D was just a few years away from retirement at the beginning of the initiative. While supportive of Six Sigma in public, behind closed doors was another matter. He often belittled the initiative to his employees in private meetings by saying, "I've seen every one of these improvement initiatives come and go in the past. Six Sigma is no different." Without commitment from their leader, employees in bureau D weren't able to make a single improvement to their processes. The productivity level in bureau D remained static at 90 contracts per month.

The employees of bureau C are extremely frustrated. The information they receive from bureau B is in a format that makes it difficult for them to do their job in a prompt manner. The different types of contracts they receive are not similar in any manner whatsoever, and, therefore, employees in bureau C must hunt for the data they need. The manager of bureau C tried to participate in the Six Sigma initiative but she found herself swamped with a perpetual backlog. There were several important contracts under way, and the director had expressed his desire that those contracts be accelerated and completed as soon as possible. The manager of bureau C assembled a solid team to participate in the Six Sigma training but was not able to interact with the team other than to attend the kickoff meeting and pledge her support. Her words were sincere, but in the weeks and months following the initial meeting the team was not able to allocate much time to their Six Sigma project because they were too busy accelerating the contracts the director had identified as a priority for the organization. Six Sigma had little effect in bureau C, and productivity levels did not rise above the baseline of 70 contracts per month. See Figure 10.2.

At the end of the fiscal year, the director was anxious to communicate the results of his Six Sigma initiative to the house appropriations committee

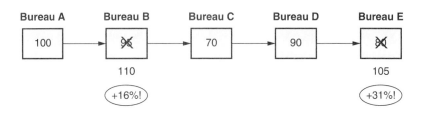

Figure 10.2   Example improvement results.

with the hope of winning over several members who had been vocally critical of the agency's operations in the past. He ordered his staff to gather together measures of the agency's performance for the past year. To his dismay, he discovered that the number of contracts processed in the current fiscal year was nearly identical to the number processed in the prior year—840. Disheartened, the director concluded that Six Sigma simply doesn't work in government organizations.

This example illustrates the problem with improvement initiatives in most organizations: they are not controlled within the framework of a management system. Had management in the fictional organization reviewed the operation of the system as a whole, they would have identified bureau C as the bottleneck of the entire process. With further investigation they would have identified the problem with the interface between bureau B and bureau C cited in the example. A cross-functional team could have been assembled to identify simple solutions to improve this interface. If productivity could have been improved to 80 contracts per month, the system output would have increased by 10 contracts per month, or 120 contracts per year. A 10 percent gain in productivity could have been realized with a minimum of time and effort.

The moral of the story should be clear: build an effective management system first, and then use it to look for opportunities to improve operations.

CLAUSE 4.2.1: GENERAL REQUIREMENTS

Clause 4.2.1 contains the documentation requirements of the ISO 9001 standard. The following documents comprise the organization's quality management system:

1. Quality policy and quality objectives

2. Quality manual

3. Documented procedures required by the ISO 9001 standard

    a. Document control procedure

    b. Control of records procedure

    c. Internal audit procedure

    d. Control of nonconforming product/service procedure

    e. Corrective action procedure

    f. Preventive action procedure

4. Any documents necessary to ensure effective planning, operation, and control of the organization's processes

5. Records required by the ISO 9001 standard

At the IDOT, the real challenge wasn't so much the creation of new documentation; it was working to bring our existing documentation into compliance. The Department has literally hundreds of manuals, procedures, and other publications. One of the mistakes we made was that we didn't first try to determine where we were already meeting the requirements of the standard. We made an assumption that many changes would be necessary to meet the requirements of the ISO 9001 standard. We failed to understand that IDOT has been in existence for nearly one hundred years, and during that time some very smart individuals have worked within the agency and have created and revised effective procedures and controls to ensure high standards of quality. Everyone stumbles into the truth occasionally. The key is to canvass the organization and discover those areas where conformance to ISO 9001 requirements already exists. During this investigation, you will likely encounter processes or activities that could help the organization meet the requirements of the standard with just a few tweaks. You'll soon discover that what is really needed is a single document that ties the entire organization together. Fortunately, the ISO 9001 standard can help.

CLAUSE 4.2.2: QUALITY MANUAL

Clause 4.2.2 contains the following requirements for an organization's quality manual:

1. Must contain the scope of the quality management system, including the details of and justification for any exclusions from the requirements of the standard.

2. Must contain or reference the procedures that have been established for the quality management system

3. Must contain a description of the interaction between the processes of the quality management system

Technically speaking, a one-page quality manual could meet the requirement of the ISO 9001 standard. On the practical side, this probably isn't the best approach for your organization. If you are seeking certification to the ISO 9001 standard, a registrar will be visiting your organization soon to determine how your organization addresses the requirements of the standard. A properly developed quality manual can go a long way toward explaining your management system to your employees and your registrar.

At IDOT, we created a quality manual that is homologous to the ISO 9001 standard. In other words, the sections of the quality manual mirror the clauses of the standard. The quality manual explains how IDOT meets each specific requirement of the ISO 9001 standard. How can you accomplish this task in your own organization? Conduct a gap analysis. Purchase a copy of the ISO 9001 standard and review the many requirements. Create a simple matrix and rephrase each requirement of the standard in the form of a question. Your matrix might look something like Table 10.1.

Find yourself a small group of ambitious employees with an inquisitive streak, hand them copies of the matrix, and empower them to talk to anyone and everyone in the organization to determine the answers to the

Table 10.1   Example gap analysis matrix.

Clause	Requirement	Answer
5.5.1	How are responsibilities and authorities defined and communicated within our organization?	Job descriptions and organizational charts.
5.6.1	How does top management review the performance of our organization?	A senior staff retreat is held each year.
6.4	How is the work environment needed for quality determined and managed within our organization?	Business Services works with offices to develop annual operating budgets. Needs are prioritized by top management.
7.2.3	What arrangements has our organization implemented to ensure effective communication with our customers? Do these arrangements include: • Product/service information? • Enquiries, contracts, or order handling, including amendments? • Customer feedback, including customer complaints?	• Complaints are tracked by the communications center. • Written correspondence is tracked by the executive office. • E-mail inquiries are tracked by External Affairs. • The annual program is posted on the organization's Web site. • Information on individual projects is available through the regional offices.

matrix questions. You will likely be surprised at the level of conformance of your organization to the requirements of the ISO 9001 standard. There will likely be some gaps where the organization's management system does not meet the requirements of the standard, but identifying areas of conformance first will help you build momentum early in the process. You will still have plenty of work ahead of you in bringing the organization into conformance with the requirements of the standard, but you will avoid redundant activity in areas where you are already in conformance with the requirements of the standard.

As an alternative, you can also purchase a copy of the ISO 9004:2000 standard and utilize the self-assessment provided in Annex A of the document. It's a bit more comprehensive than the 9001 standard, as 9004 covers many more areas of the organization. It's an excellent exercise and one that will pay dividends down the line. More discussion regarding the execution of a gap analysis is presented in Chapter 14.

CLAUSE 5.6: MANAGEMENT REVIEW

Clause 5.6 of the ISO 9001 standard requires top management to review the quality management system at planned intervals to ensure its continuing suitability, adequacy, and effectiveness. This review is intended to be a comprehensive assessment of the performance of the organization, and the standard has specific requirements for what areas must be covered during this review. Records of management reviews are required to be maintained, and this includes any decisions and actions related to improvement of the quality management system and its processes, improvement of products or services related to customer requirements, and resource needs.

At IDOT, we viewed management review not as an event but as a process. In order to better align the requirements of the standard with our own organizational structure, we integrated our management review process into our strategic planning process. Strategic reviews are conducted by top management on a semiannual basis. These reviews meet all of the requirements of clause 5.6 of the standard and also allow us to review our strategic plan to determine if revisions need to be made. Revisions or adjustments to the agency's strategic goals and objectives are communicated to the offices and divisions of the agency in the form of objectives, targets, and improvement goals. Managers at the operational level translate the objectives, targets, and improvement goals into bureau, section, and individual objectives and develop measurements and targets to support the achievement of these goals. Reviews are conducted at the operational level twice annually to determine process effectiveness and to identify opportunities for

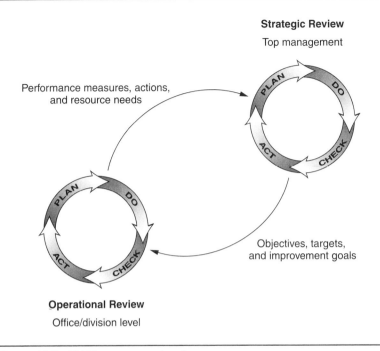

Figure 10.3 IDOT management review process.

improvement. Performance measures, actions, and resulting resource needs are communicated to top management, and the review cycle begins again. See Figure 10.3.

By viewing management review as a process instead of an event, IDOT has been able to better manage interrelated work activities and processes as a system. The strategic reviews ensure that improvements to individual activities, processes, or areas are not undertaken without a determination of the potential impact to the entire system, that resource needs identified by offices and divisions of the Department are tied to measurable outcomes, and that operational goals and objectives are properly aligned with strategic goals and objectives.

CLAUSE 6.1: PROVISION OF RESOURCES

Clause 6.1 of the ISO 9001 standard requires that the organization determine and provide the resources needed to implement and maintain the quality management system and continually improve its effectiveness, and to enhance customer satisfaction by meeting customer requirements. To best accomplish this requirement, provision of resources should be tied to the organization's management review process. At IDOT, resource needs are communicated to top management through operational reviews at the office/division level. Resource needs are determined based on the objectives, targets, and improvement goals identified by top management during strategic reviews.

CLAUSE 8.2.2: INTERNAL AUDITS

Clause 8.2.2 of the ISO 9001 standard requires the organization to conduct internal audits at planned intervals to determine whether the quality management system conforms to the requirements of documented procedures and the ISO 9001 standard and is properly implemented and maintained. At IDOT we quickly discovered that our internal audit process was probably the single most important element in successful implementation of the ISO 9001 standard requirements.

Many organizations suffer what I like to refer to as an "execution gap." An execution gap is a chasm between the strategic vision and goals of the organization and actual performance. IDOT was no exception. Over the years many excellent strategies for improvement had been identified and initiated, but with the ever-increasing demands of day-to-day operations, action plans to implement improvement strategies were often set aside to handle "real work" with the understanding that "we'll tackle this when things settle down a bit." Seasoned leaders understand that things will never "settle down." There are always fires to put out and rush projects to complete, so primary priorities get accomplished first and secondary priorities get accomplished never. Improvement initiatives are almost always launched with good intentions, but successful execution requires a bit more than quixotic hope; it requires a rearrangement of priorities. We discovered that the internal audit process required by ISO 9001 forced us to *follow through on our good intentions.* By continually reviewing processes and areas of the quality management system, we were able to identify areas where implementation had not been successful and initiate actions to improve conformance.

There are many different ways to implement an ISO 9001 internal audit program, and there are benefits and costs inherent to each approach. Institutionalizing an internal audit program by creating full-time positions within the organization is arguably the best way to ensure a consistent and effective approach to auditing. The downside of such an approach is that internal resistance can be created when an office is established within an organization with the singular purpose of assessing the performance of other offices. Outsourcing the internal audit program can reduce the workload required of staff while increasing the objectivity of the audit. The cost of outsourcing audits can be costly though—especially if your organization is considering certification of your management system, which will require further use of external audits. A middle-of-the-road approach consists of identifying a team of volunteers within the organization, training them on ISO 9001 requirements and internal audit procedures, and empowering them to conduct audit interviews and prepare audit findings. Using a team of volunteers from within the organization to conduct internal audits exacts a cost in time, resources, and productivity. If employees are busy auditing, they are unable to complete their required responsibilities and authorities. In order to implement such an approach within an organization scarce on resources, deliberate and careful planning is necessary to ensure that employees are not engaged in audit activities during times of heavy workloads.

A volunteer approach to internal auditing was the method selected by IDOT to implement the required internal audit program within the organization. The management representative determined that semiannual audits would be the best fit for the organization, with one audit taking place during the spring and the other audit occurring in the fall. The internal audit team would review most processes of the quality management system once annually, which allowed us to effectively split up the audit load so that only approximately half of the system was audited during any one audit. This allowed us to avoid negatively impacting operations during times of heavy demand. An audit schedule was developed that assigned audits to areas during the period when workload was lowest. An internal audit procedure was developed based on guidance from the ISO 19011 standard (guidelines for quality and/or environmental management systems auditing). Areas critical to the continued integrity of the quality management system, such as management review, corrective action, and internal audits (yes, we even audit our audit program!) were reviewed during each audit along with any other areas where previous audits had identified the need for more frequent reviews due to low conformance or poor performance.

Volunteers were identified at all levels of the organization. A three-day training session was conducted a week prior to the initiation of the first audit of the year (spring audit). The internal auditor training was based on the guidelines of the ISO 19011:2004 standard. The training included a thorough review of the ISO 9001 and 19011 standards and a mock audit of a fictional company to allow participants to implement audit interview techniques and concepts taught in the class. Participants were debriefed and provided constructive feedback on their performance and suggestions for improvement. Effectiveness of the internal auditor training was evaluated with the administration of a comprehensive written test. Only participants who answered a minimum of 70 percent of the questions correctly were allowed to participate as members of the internal audit team. Once the training was completed, a member of the team was selected to be the lead auditor. The lead auditor is responsible for coordinating the audit, assigning audit interviews to audit team members, and documenting the results of the audit in a final report for top management.

All internal audits at IDOT are initiated with an opening meeting of all areas to review the scope and schedule of the internal audit as well as discuss procedures that govern the internal audit program. Audits are conducted over the course of a 30-day period. Audit teams are assigned to specific areas to review processes and instructed to contact management in those areas to determine a date to schedule the audit that best accommodates the schedules of all involved parties. During the audit, the team discusses each process or activity with appropriate personnel and reviews objective evidence in the form of records, data, measurements, or observations to determine the answer to four basic questions:

1. Is the process identified and appropriately defined?

2. Are responsibilities assigned?

3. Are the procedures implemented and maintained?

4. Is the process effective in achieving the required results?

The audit team also reviews process documents to ensure they are being properly controlled, personnel records to ensure that process employees have the necessary training and skills to complete their responsibilities, and previously completed corrective and preventive actions (see Chapter 11) to ensure that the actions taken were effective and properly implemented. When the audit team encounters instances of nonconformance, audit findings are generated. The audit team is also empowered to identify potential problems and opportunities for improvement.

Once the audit interviews are completed, a closing meeting is conducted and the results of the audits are reviewed with all areas. An internal audit report is generated containing a summary of the audit activities conducted and the individual findings of the internal audit teams. Corrective actions are required for all nonconformities documented by the internal audit team, and corrective action requests are issued soon after the closing meeting. Offices are given 30 days to complete an investigation of the issue and submit a proposed corrective action plan. Preventive actions are not mandated but strongly recommended for all observations and opportunities for improvement documented by the internal audit team. The final task remaining is an evaluation of the performance of the audit team by the lead auditor. The feedback received on the audit team's performance provides the input into the improvement of the next internal auditor training class.

Examples of internal audit forms are available in Appendix B.

SUMMARY

- All work is a system of interrelated processes.

- An effective management system will help top management identify opportunities for improvement using tools like Six Sigma.

- Work first to bring existing documentation into compliance with the requirements of the ISO 9001 standard.

- A properly designed quality manual will provide a great tool to explain your quality system to your employees as well as your registrar.

- Management review is a process—not an event.

- A properly designed management review process should include reviews at different levels of the organization.

- Provision of resources should be tied directly to the organization's management review process.

- An effective internal audit process will drive improved conformance to the requirements of the management system.

- There are many different ways to implement an ISO 9001 internal audit program. Compare the benefits and costs of each approach to find the best fit for your organization.

- Use the ISO 19011 standard to develop your audit program.

- Use your corrective action system to address internal audit findings.

11

Continual Improvement

*Perfection of means and confusion of goals seem—in
my opinion—to characterize our age.*

—Albert Einstein, *Out of My Later Years*

INTRODUCTION

There is an interesting paralysis that seems to infect many public-sector
organizations. Since most government agencies are required to enforce
compliance to statutory and regulatory requirements, a culture of compliance seems to flourish in this environment. The theory goes that since
the public-sector organization is enforcing compliance to requirements, the
organization must also "do things right." This is a desirable characteristic in
some ways, but there is a tremendous downside. Inside an organization with
such strong mores employees often become afraid to make mistakes. When
this type of fear takes hold, risk management takes on a twisted meaning.
Organizations with strong cultures of compliance often attempt to mitigate
every conceivable risk to product/service quality. Have you ever wondered
how bureaucracy is created? I can explain it to you in one sentence: *the
attempt to mitigate for every conceivable contingency is the mother of all
bureaucracy.* Make a note—you heard it here first, folks.

The bitter irony of this group mind-set is that the thing that is most feared
actually occurs: employees make mistakes—lots of them! Management is
aghast at the results. "Employees aren't following procedures? We must
make sure they understand the importance of conformance!" A predictable
knee-jerk reaction ensues and management devises new controls that they
are certain will improve conformance to procedures. This vicious cycle con-
tinues to spawn more and more stringent controls as the organization slowly
slips closer and closer toward an abyss of unmanageable bureaucracy.

This approach is sadly misdirected. Mistakes don't typically happen because employees don't understand the importance of conforming to procedures; most mistakes happen because employees are hamstrung by archaic processes. Why are they hamstrung by archaic processes? Because no one has the courage to change them. Innovation creates risk—remember? As a result, employees in public-sector organizations often come to see their responsibility within a job as executing a process that has been given to them. Managers feel their responsibility is to ensure the integrity of that process at all times and drive compliance constantly. The fallacy of this perspective of course is that no one should ever be brought into any organization to simply execute a process. They should be hired to achieve an *objective*. A process is simply one way to achieve an objective. Processes *can and should change* as new information is received and better ways of achieving the objective are determined.

W. Edwards Deming recognized the futility of trying to inspect quality into a process. During his many years of quality consulting, he found that only 6% of problems related to a process have an assignable cause. Deming found that the other 94% of the problems are inherent in the process itself. In other words, 94% of the problems encountered in a given process are *built into the process*. The only way to eliminate these types of problems is to make fundamental changes to the process. In Deming's view, the dizzying array of inspections, approvals, and reviews instituted by risk-averse organizations are counterproductive. Not only do these approaches decrease efficiency and productivity, they usually *increase* the number of errors that occur. In his book *Out of the Crisis*, Deming documented a Monte Carlo experiment he conducted many times during lectures using a funnel and a marble to demonstrate the disaster in quality that often occurs when a well-meaning manager tampers with a process in a reactive manner. Deming would do 50 drops of the marble and mark the spot where the marble came to rest. As you can imagine, a random scattering of marks resulted. He would then ask a member of the audience to perform another run of 50 drops but this time he instructed the audience member to adjust the funnel after each drop using the position of the point where the last marble came to rest. Each location was marked as in the first sequence. At the end of the second run, Deming had the audience member compare the scattering of marks that resulted from his adjustment to Deming's initial run. The second run showed an explosion in the amount of variation from the initial fixed position. Through the performance of this simple experiment, Deming demonstrated the futility of managers trying to adjust a process with additional controls. The end result is generally worse than if the manager had simply left the process alone. In Deming's view, management needs to stop focusing on assigning causes to every fault and blemish that occurs and instead focus their attention on continually improving the system. Continual improvement is the focus of this chapter.

CLAUSE 8.3: NONCONFORMING PRODUCT/SERVICE

The poet John Keats said that failure is, in a way, "the highway to success," reasoning that each encounter with what is false leads us closer to the truth. Clearly John Keats understood that learning from our mistakes is a powerful catalyst to change and improvement. If we are going to learn from our mistakes, we must remember them! By keeping records of what we are not doing right, we can identify what must be changed in order to improve. Clause 8.3 of the ISO 9001 standard establishes the requirement that the organization keep records of nonconformities. A documented procedure is required to define the controls and related responsibilities and authorities for dealing with these nonconformities. The ISO 9001 standard requires that these nonconformities be addressed in one of four ways:

- *By taking action to eliminate the detected nonconformity.* The organization may correct the problem through rework or reprocessing.

- *By authorizing its use, release, or acceptance under concession by a relevant authority, or where applicable, by the customer.* A relevant authority (or the customer) may accept the nonconforming product or service in exchange for a discount.

- *By taking action to preclude its original use or application.* The organization may scrap the nonconforming work and start again from scratch.

- *By taking action appropriate to the effects of the nonconformity when the nonconformity is detected after delivery or use has started.* If the nonconformity is discovered after delivery of the product or after the service has been provided, an organization may replace the defective product or redo the service at no charge to the customer.

Maintaining records of what we have not done right provides us with a great opportunity to analyze this data and identify changes to our processes and procedures that can improve the ability of the organization to meet customer requirements. Recording nonconformities does not need to be an onerous task. It can be completed very easily with a form, by the use of a log, or by use of electronic means. All that is needed is to clearly identify the nonconformity and identify the nature of the nonconformity, how it was addressed, and who addressed it. When reviewing nonconformities, it is important to remember the results of Deming's experiment with the funnel: 94% of nonconformities that occur are built into the process, and tampering with a stable process can lead to disastrous results.

For a further discussion of the analysis of nonconformities and the opportunities for improvement that may result from such an analysis, please see Chapter 12.

FOUR MODES OF FIX

The ISO 9001 standard recognizes four modes of fix:

- *Correction:* action to eliminate a detected nonconformity.

- *Corrective action:* action to eliminate the cause of a detected nonconformity or other undesirable situation.

- *Preventive action:* action to eliminate the cause of a potential nonconformity or other undesirable potential situation.

- *Continual improvement:* recurring activity to increase the ability to fulfill requirements.

In order to demonstrate the application of these four modes, let's consider the process of contract processing. Action taken to correct a single contract that is nonconforming would be considered a correction. Someone made a mistake and someone else fixes the mistake. This is appropriate when the error is an isolated incident with low ramifications to overall quality or customer satisfaction. If there appears to be a systemic problem (that is, the same problem keeps occurring) and quality and/or customer satisfaction has been compromised, corrective action should be applied. Corrective action would involve a more rigorous investigation to determine the root cause of the nonconformity and implementation of action that would eliminate the cause of the nonconformity.

Preventive action might be initiated if it is noticed that the standard language within the contract is vague and there could be misunderstanding of what is required. In this case, a problem has not yet occurred, but it has been decided that the potential exists for errors to occur, so it is appropriate to initiate preventive action. Continual improvement might be applied if the organization desires to convert the existing contract template from a Word document to an electronic contract generator with the goal of improving the speed with which contracts are processed.

The ISO 9001 standard contains very specific requirements for the organization to observe when fixing problems. Requirements for correction were previously identified in the preceding section (clause 8.3: Nonconforming product/service). The ISO 9001 standard requirements for the processes of corrective action, preventive action, and continual improvement are the subject of the remainder of this chapter.

CLAUSE 8.5.2:
CORRECTIVE ACTION

Corrective action is an often misunderstood requirement of the ISO 9001 standard. That's because we too often seek to "correct" a symptom of a problem instead of addressing the real, deep-down cause. It's an entirely human trait to treat the "symptom" of the problem rather than the root cause because the symptom is what is so readily observable. We can't cure the common cold, so we treat the runny nose and sneezing. There is the old Henny Youngman joke about a patient who tells his doctor "it hurts when I do this." The doctor's solution is to tell the patient "Then don't do that!"

How often have we told our employees "don't do that"? Probably more often than we'd care to admit. An audit finding that reveals *employees are not following the documented design procedure* is often addressed by the issuance of a stern warning that *employees not following the required design procedure may face disciplinary action.* This response, though typical in many organizations, treats the symptom without looking at the cause of the problem. Telling people to follow the procedure is fast, it's easy, and it makes sense to most people. Unfortunately, the root cause of the problem is still there and has not been addressed. The question remains, "Why are these employees not following the required procedure?"

The ISO 9001 standard recognizes this human tendency to head in the wrong direction on problem solving, and that's why the standard requires a documented corrective action procedure. Clause 8.5.2 of the standard requires the organization to take action to eliminate the cause of nonconformities in order to prevent recurrence. A documented procedure for corrective action is required and must define the requirements for:

a. Reviewing nonconformities (including customer complaints)

b. Determining the causes of nonconformities

c. Evaluating the need for action to ensure that nonconformities do not recur

d. Determining and implementing action needed

e. Records of the results of actions taken

f. Reviewing the effectiveness of the corrective action taken

The main point here is the requirement that corrective action *eliminate the cause of nonconformities.* This requires a *root cause* investigation (an investigation to determine the beginning event that caused the problem to occur). At its most basic level, root cause investigation is little more than continuing to ask the question, "Why did this happen?" With this in mind, our earlier example of a typical audit finding can be further examined:

Employees are not following the documented design procedure.

Why did this happen?

The documented design procedure has not been updated to adequately reflect the current process design employees are required to follow.

Why did this happen?

AASHTO guidelines changed January 1, 2009, which required revisions to be made to the design procedure. A revised copy was submitted for approval six weeks ago but has not yet been approved.

Why did this happen?

A change in procedure requires four approval signatures. Typically, revisions to official procedures require an average of eight weeks to process.

Why did this happen?

Root cause: The current system for updating and communicating procedures is cumbersome and inefficient, which may cause the written procedures to be out of date.

How about that? Instead of threatening our employees with disciplinary action for *trying to do a good job,* we now understand that the root cause is an inefficient document control system. An effective fix of the document control system will ensure that this problem never happens again. Now we have not only fixed the problem in the design area, but we've eliminated the potential for the problem to occur in other areas of the organization. Of course, this is a very simple example chosen to illustrate the root cause investigation methodology. Most problems are much more complex and require the input of experienced, well-trained staff and a great deal of time to determine their root cause(s).

It should be pretty obvious by this point that true corrective action requires the allocation of some serious resources. Employees engaged in problem solving of this magnitude aren't completing regular job assignments. Solutions to root causes can potentially cost thousands of dollars—perhaps more. For this reason, it's important that organizations develop qualifications to determine when true corrective action is necessary and when a simple band-aid solution (correction) is warranted. At IDOT, we use the qualifications shown in Figure 11.1 to determine the need to implement corrective action.

Once we've decided to pursue corrective action, determined the root cause of the problem, and implemented the recommended corrective action to eliminate the cause of the problem, there is still work to be done. After an appropriate amount of time has passed, we need to go back and determine whether the corrective action implemented was actually effective. If we can verify that the corrective action was effective by reviewing measurements or simply observing the activity, then we can close out the corrective action process. If we are unable to confirm that the corrective action is indeed effective, we need to go back to square one and start the investigation all over again.

To summarize: truly effective corrective action identifies the *cause* of the problem and eliminates it to prevent recurrence. Ineffective corrective action merely masks the "symptoms" of the problem and exposes the organization to greater problems farther down the road. A systematic approach

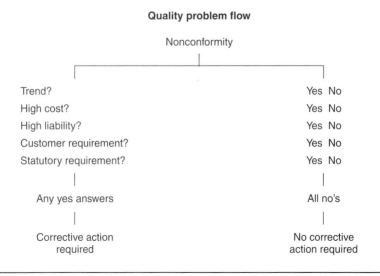

Figure 11.1 Example corrective action qualifications.

to corrective action can pay big dividends down the line by eliminating the causes of problems that sap the organization's resources. Things will really start to improve when your organization embraces the concept of preventing problems before they occur.

CLAUSE 8.5.3: PREVENTIVE ACTION

Clause 8.5.3 of the standard requires the organization to take action to eliminate the causes of potential nonconformities to prevent occurrence. As with corrective action, a documented procedure for preventive action is required and must define the requirements for:

a. Reviewing potential nonconformities and their causes

b. Evaluating the need for action to prevent occurrence of nonconformities

c. Determining and implementing action needed

d. Records of the results of actions taken

e. Reviewing the effectiveness of the preventive action taken

Preventive action is similar in execution to corrective action, but the emphasis is on the identification of causes of potential problems.

Implementation of effective preventive action can be an excellent way to minimize your organization's exposure to negative risk. At IDOT, the implementation of preventive action is often tied to action items developed during risk management exercises. A good example of this approach is the risk management exercise we implemented in 2009 to identify potential risks to the delivery of the American Recovery and Reinvestment Act (ARRA) program in Illinois. To aid in the identification and assessment of risks, we utilized a failure mode and effects analysis (FMEA). We focused the analysis on identifying potential modes of failure that could lead to the non-accomplishment of the eight accountability objectives of the ARRA. These potential modes of failure (or risks) can also be thought of as potential causes of quality problems. Each potential cause (risk) identified was assessed to determine the severity of a potential occurrence (how big of a problem will it be if it occurs), the likelihood of occurrence (how likely is it this problem will occur), and the likelihood that existing controls would not identify the problem (how likely is it that the problem will be detected?). The assessment used a numerical scale (1 = very low, 2 = low, 3 = moderate, 4 = high) and the input of senior managers from all areas of IDOT. The overall assessment ratings for each category—*severity* (S), *occurrence* (O), and *detection* (D)—were an average of all individual ratings. The category ratings for each potential cause were multiplied to provide a risk priority number (S × O × D = RPN). The RPN generated was assessed against a matrix that had been previously developed to determine the overall level of risk for each item. Any potential cause for which two of the rating categories were identified as *high* was identified as a high risk overall on the matrix. See Figure 11.2.

All moderate and high-risk items (potential causes) were reviewed to determine which of four main risk management strategies was most appropriate:

Accept: do nothing and accept the risk.

Transfer: make the risk the responsibility of someone else.

Eliminate: take action to eliminate the risk.

Mitigate: reduce the risk with appropriate controls.

8	16	24	32	40	48	56	64
7	14	21	28	35	42	49	56
6	12	18	24	30	36	42	48
5	10	15	20	25	30	35	40
4	8	12	16	20	24	28	32
3	6	9	12	15	18	21	24
2	4	6	8	10	12	14	16
1	2	3	4	5	6	7	8

= High risk

= Intermediate risk

= Low risk

Figure 11.2   Risk matrix.

Once an appropriate risk management strategy was identified for each risk, action items were generated and tracked to ensure implementation. Once implementation was complete, verification was assigned to an employee unassociated with the risk management exercise who reviewed the action item to ensure that it was properly implemented and effective in achieving the goal of the risk management strategy employed. For instance, an employee who was assigned to review an action item that was generated to eliminate one of the identified risks was required to answer the following question, "Was the risk actually eliminated by the action taken, or does risk still exist in this area?" Action items that were not properly implemented or not effective in achieving the identified strategy were reassigned for investigation and development of further preventive actions. Action items that were found to be properly implemented and effective in achieving the desired results were closed, and records were maintained.

CLAUSE 8.5.1: CONTINUAL IMPROVEMENT

This is where the rubber meets the road. So far we have discussed the need for the quality policy, quality objectives, internal audits, analysis of data, process measurements, management review, and corrective and preventive action. Clause 8.5.1 requires that the organization use all of these resources to continually improve the effectiveness of the quality management system. It's important to remember that the standard is based on the plan–do–check–act principle, shown in Figure 11.3. Applying this principle to this clause, we can create a simple yet powerful process for continual improvement of our organization.

The implementation of this cycle is critical to the success of an ISO 9001 certification effort. By focusing the efforts of management toward initiating and sustaining this cycle of continual improvement, you will begin to see systemic improvement to the ability of the organization to meet requirements and exceed customer expectations. Don't be deceived by the simplicity of this concept; implementing this cycle in your organization will dramatically improve the quality and efficiency of operations.

It is common in organizations seeking certification for leaders to focus much of their efforts at the process level to ensure that things are done right the first time. While this is an admirable goal, it results in spotty improvements within the organization that often do not help the organization achieve its strategic goals. While individual improvements are important and are to be encouraged, they should not be undertaken without a thorough assessment of their impact on the entire system. An improvement

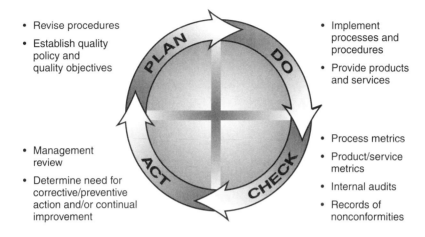

- Revise procedures
- Establish quality policy and quality objectives

- Management review
- Determine need for corrective/preventive action and/or continual improvement

- Implement processes and procedures
- Provide products and services

- Process metrics
- Product/service metrics
- Internal audits
- Records of nonconformities

Figure 11.3 ISO 9001–based process for continual improvement.

in one area that causes delays in another is not an improvement. It may help someone get promoted but it certainly does not aid the organization in reaching its goals. Implementation of a process for continual improvement at the organizational level is a powerful tool for identifying opportunities for improvement and allocating scarce resources where they can be used best to help the organization meet the requirements of customers and exceed their expectations.

SUMMARY

- An overemphasis on compliance to procedures can often cause employees to fear making mistakes. This is counterproductive to the concept of continual improvement.

- No one should be hired to merely execute a process; they should be hired to achieve an *objective*.

- Processes can and should change as new information is received and better ways of achieving objectives are determined.

- Attempts by managers to adjust processes based on individual results most often induces a reduction in quality and efficiency.

- Recording and analyzing nonconformities can be a powerful tool for identifying changes to processes and procedures.

- The ISO 9001 standard recognizes four modes of "fix": correction, corrective action, preventive action, and continual improvement.

- Corrective action eliminates the cause of the problem to prevent recurrence.

- Preventive action eliminates the cause of potential problems to prevent occurrence.

- Implementation of the plan–do–check–act principle along with the requirements of clause 8.5.1 will create a simple yet powerful process for continual improvement of an organization.

- Improvements to individual areas must never be implemented without a thorough assessment of the impact of these improvements on the overall system.

12

Factual Approach to Decision Making

A little Learning is a dang'rous Thing;
Drink deep, or taste not the Pierian Spring:
There shallow Draughts intoxicate the Brain,
And drinking largely sobers us again.

—Alexander Pope, *An Essay on Criticism*

INTRODUCTION

When I was a kid, I wanted to be an orchestral conductor. From my perspective, the conductor had the cushiest job in the entire world. All he had to do was show up for an hour or so and simply wave his baton around while the symphony played on. It wasn't until I became an adult that I realized that it's really a difficult job. Getting 75 to 100 people all thinking on the same wavelength is extremely challenging. The one to two hours you hear at a concert is the culmination of hundreds of hours of practice. The conductor must continually analyze the output of the symphony over and over again and provide feedback on what needs to be improved. The conductor may order a little more emphasis by the trumpets in one section, and then may tell the woodwinds to soften their tone in another section. The point is, the conductor controls the output of the symphony by constantly measuring the performance (by listening), analyzing it (by comparing it to the musical score), and improving the symphony's performance by giving them feedback.

In the same way, top management has a role that is equally as challenging as the orchestral conductor's role. They have to synchronize the efforts of all the employees in the organization toward the achievement of the organization's mission. Think about it for a second. In your own organization, can you remember instances when the "woodwinds" jumped in way too soon? Do you recall times when the "trumpet section" missed their cue and came in too late? Of course you do—we hear about them all the time. They sound a little different: "Project construction is delayed because the necessary railroad coordination wasn't completed on time" or "Project design was completed before environmental coordination was finalized, requiring major revisions to plans."

In order to be effective, top management must have critical measurements being relayed to them so they can analyze that information and improve the overall performance of the organization. They are in a position to see the entire symphony in action and can understand how each section contributes to the overall performance of the musical piece. For a conductor, the measurement part is simple; the maestro only needs to listen. For top management in a complex organization, it's a little more difficult. Most organizations have hundreds of processes, so the question on everyone's mind is "Which ones need to be measured?" The answer can only be determined by trial and error. CEOs of public corporations often measure return on investment, current market share, profit margin, and operating cycle times. Nonprofit leaders tend to concentrate more on statistics relating to level of service (percentage of roads in acceptable condition, customer satisfaction indices, and so on).

The important thing to remember is that the measurements need to be specific to the organization and *they must be broad enough to quickly transmit the performance of the overall organization to top management.* The intent behind the principle of *factual approach to decision making* is to provide top management with a "dashboard" that can be used to quickly spot minor problems before they become major issues.

FACTUAL VERSUS ANECDOTAL APPROACH

In 1998, the Illinois Department of Transportation kicked off a strategic planning initiative with the goal of improving the agency's performance by the establishment of strategic goals and organizational performance measurements. This initiative led directly to the establishment of the ISO 9001 certification program. Before the days of strategic planning and ISO 9001, IDOT (like most public-sector organizations) was managed by the old standby—no news is good news. In other words, top management allocated resources based on complaints. The division or office that yelled the loudest received additional resources. This is a classic example of an anecdotal approach to decision making. Judgments were not made based on the analysis of data and information but rather on personal observation. It was a lot like a weatherman making a prediction based on what he saw outside the window of the weather station rather than using satellite, radar, and temperature data to create an accurate forecast.

When metrics were established with the strategic planning initiative and the ISO 9001 certification program, management began to use data and facts to support more effective decision making. Old habits die hard, and the agency still struggles at times with the effective use of data and information, but as each year goes by more and more decisions are based on the analysis of hard factual information. Today we try to live by the words of W. Edwards Deming: "In God we trust. All others bring data."

GOVERNMENT AGENCIES WOULD RATHER DEFEND PERFORMANCE

The use of measures in government agencies is not a radical concept. As discussed in Chapter 2, many of the concepts of quality management were introduced by the United States government during World War II. What is truly curious is the way measures are used in public-sector organizations. Measures are most often used in government agencies to *defend* performance, not improve it. While at first blush this phenomenon seems backwards, a more thoughtful analysis should conclude that this approach makes enormous good sense. IDOT is an executive agency, meaning that it falls under the control of the office of the governor. In this way, the governor is like the chief executive officer of a large, multidisciplinary corporation, and IDOT is simply one division of that corporation. Once every four years, our CEO must undergo an intense, months-long job interview with the shareholders (who in this case happen to be the citizens of the great state of Illinois). It has been suggested that the number one priority for a first-term governor is to win a second term and that he or she begin campaigning for a second term the day after the inauguration. The implementation of a wide variety of measures ensures that the story told will always be positive; after all, it's rare for even the worst organizations not to do some things right. The pressure to "spin" these measurements is enormous, and this phenomenon is detrimental to the growth and improvement of an organization.

The importance of measurable objectives has been stressed throughout this entire book, and this chapter is no exception. It's not important to have hundreds or thousands of measures; what is important is that the organization develops measures that *support the achievement of the organization's overall quality objectives.* Setting clear quality objectives for the organization to achieve eliminates the ability to "spin" measures and keeps the organization focused on finding ways to improve performance rather than defend it. Furthermore, a good set of measures that are designed to support the achievement of the organization's quality objectives is a powerful tool for allocating resources based on demonstrated need. By using measures to identify areas where additional resources need to be deployed, top management can tie the allocation of resources to measurable outcomes.

CLAUSE 8.2.3: MONITORING AND MEASUREMENT OF PROCESSES

Clause 8.2.3 of the ISO 9001 standard requires the organization to apply suitable methods for monitoring and, where applicable, measurement of management system processes. The methods for monitoring and measurement of processes are not specified, but whatever approach is used must demonstrate the ability of the process to achieve planned results. What are planned results? In a word—objectives. The standard does not require that all processes must be measured. However, since we understand that measurable objectives are the engine that drives organizations toward success, it makes sense that the use of process measures will drive improved performance. For the overall success of the management system, it is recommended that measurements be established for most processes. There will always be instances where measurement of certain processes is not possible. In these instances, it is permissible to develop methods of monitoring the process. Regardless of the method employed, the intent of the requirement is to use facts and data to make effective decisions.

CLAUSE 8.2.4: MONITORING AND MEASUREMENT OF PRODUCT/SERVICE

Clause 8.2.4 of the ISO 9001 standard requires the organization to monitor and measure the characteristics of products and services to ensure that requirements have been met. Evidence of conformity with acceptance criteria must be retained, and records must indicate the person(s) who authorized release of the product/service. This requirement deals with direct measurements of the product/service against requirements.

CLAUSE 8.4: ANALYSIS OF DATA

Now that we have established measurements, we must collect and analyze these data to identify where continual improvement of the effectiveness of the quality management system can be made. Clause 8.4 of the ISO 9001 standard requires that the organization collect and analyze data and information related to customer satisfaction, conformity to product requirements, characteristics and trends of processes and products, and suppliers. The output of this analysis should provide opportunities for corrective and preventive action, and also continual improvement of the system.

Analysis of data can be simple or it can be complex. The method employed depends on the type of information being produced. Two common techniques utilized at IDOT are Shewhart control charts and Pareto analysis. Shewhart control charts are named after Walter Shewhart and are a great tool for identifying the degree of process variation. Reducing variation in process output leads to more consistent results.

Figure 12.1 is an example of a Shewhart control chart developed to track the number of days required to process contract changes. The number of days required for each contract change is plotted on the chart. Elementary statistical analysis was performed to determine the mean and the standard deviation. In this example the mean is 21.675 days and the standard deviation is 9.147 days. When using Shewhart control charts to monitor processes, the third standard deviation of the mean is generally used to establish control limits. Using the third standard deviation of the mean in this example yields an upper control limit of 49.116 days (a lower control limit is not necessary in this example). Once constructed, the chart provides a

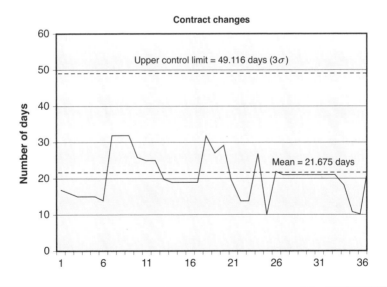

Figure 12.1   Example of a Shewhart control chart.

valuable tool for monitoring the process and identifying opportunities for improvement with the objective of minimizing variation in the process. The chart should be analyzed continually as new data are added to determine if the process is out of control or is trending in that direction. Indications that a process is out of control include:

- A single point outside the upper or lower control limits.

- Two out of three successive points on the same side of the mean and farther than 2σ from it.

- Four out of five successive points on the same side of the mean and farther than 1σ from it.

A Pareto analysis is often used as a tool for further investigation of unacceptable variation revealed by a Shewhart control chart. A Pareto analysis is so named because it is based on a principle postulated by an Italian economist named Vilfredo Pareto. Pareto proposed that approximately 80 percent of effects come from 20 percent of the causes. This is the famous 80/20 rule that has become a fundamental rule of thumb for a generation. Use of the 80/20 principle is not always appropriate in every aspect of life, but for process improvement it provides a simple means to quickly analyze a process to determine where our efforts can be best focused to facilitate improvement results. A Pareto analysis most often takes the form of ranking the causes of process variation or problems. By ranking the causes, we can analyze the data to determine where best to concentrate our efforts in order to improve the process.

Figure 12.2 is an example of a Pareto chart developed to further investigate unacceptable results from the change order process Shewhart chart in Figure 12.1. In this example, the frequency of different types of errors associated with contract change orders is identified on the chart along with a cumulative frequency. The results plotted in Figure 12.2 demonstrate that the majority of change orders (nearly 70%) are generated because of two causes: incorrect coding and design errors. By focusing our efforts on identifying solutions for these two main causes, we can vastly improve the process. Focusing on the remaining causes would provide only small improvement to the process and is arguably not the best use of our limited resources.

The American Society for Quality (ASQ) has developed a great collection of quality tools like Shewhart control charts and Pareto analysis and has free information on the correct use of them on its Web site (www.asq.org). A book called *SPC for Right-Brain Thinkers* by Lon Roberts (ASQ Quality Press, 2006) is another great resource.

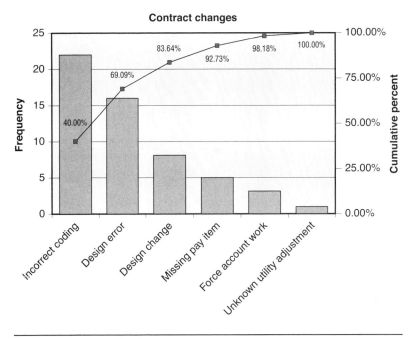

Figure 12.2   Example of a Pareto chart.

WHAT KINDS OF FACTS (DATA AND INFORMATION) SHOULD BE COLLECTED?

Many employees in public-sector organizations are mistakenly led to believe they are hired to complete a set of activities. If they are given the task of completing A + B + C + D, they often judge their performance based on the number of times they are able to complete steps A through D in a given day. A day of poor performance might be 30 cycles, a great performance might be 50 cycles, and anywhere in between is just an average day.

Intuitively, this makes sense to us. We hire people to do a job, right? While on the surface this perspective may seem correct, it is actually misguided. As stated in Chapter 11, we do not hire people to do a job; we hire people to accomplish an *objective*. Most of the processes and activities within public-sector organizations were established long ago for reasons many employees can not remember. Year in and year out, these employees continue to conduct the activity exactly the same without a second's thought to why the process was established in the first place.

The challenge for employees of public-sector organizations is to figure out the answer to the question, "What is the objective of your process?" The individual steps of the process are merely a method devised long ago to accomplish a defined objective. What was that objective? Is it still valid? Is the process still the best way to accomplish that objective? Once process objectives are defined, measurements should be developed that provide data and information that can be used to determine if those objectives are being achieved. Table 12.1 provides a few examples of objectives and measures for common processes in most organizations.

Process objectives and measurements are an important component of a successful management system. The absence of facts and information to drive allocation of resources leads to an anecdotal approach to decision

Table 12.1   Examples of process objectives and measurements.

Process	Objective	Measurement
Human resources	• Vacant positions filled quickly • Diverse, high-quality workforce	• Average number of days needed to fill vacant positions • Percentage of women and minorities as a function of overall employment • Average number of applicants per vacancy
Contract processing	• Contracts processed quickly and accurately	• Percentage of contracts processed within 30 days • Number of change orders required due to processing errors
Engineering	• Innovative projects completed on time and within budget	• Percentage of projects completed on time • Percent of change orders to total project cost • Value engineering cost savings
Training	• Provide quality training to enhance employee skills and improve job performance	• Percentage of identified training needs completed • Employee survey responses to training quality • Course evaluation scores

making. This method of management promotes the establishment of kingdoms and fiefdoms in public-sector organizations as individual divisions or offices learn to wage war on each other in the fight for resources. To the victors go the spoils, and the losers are relegated to mediocrity. This is no way to run a successful organization.

The establishment of a measurement system can help improve this condition, but unless it is tied directly to the achievement of the organization's primary objectives, conditions will soon deteriorate as individual areas learn to use measures and data to defend performance. A measurement system that is well integrated with the organization's overall objectives and goals will provide the all-important facts and data that top management requires to allocate resources based on need and to identify opportunities for improvement.

It must be remembered that no metrics are perfect. It's not important to find the perfect measurements of performance for your organization. What is critical in the development of a measurement system is that it is focused on providing information to top management that will allow them to make effective decisions when allocating scarce resources. As noted in the introduction of this chapter, an organization is much like an orchestra. The establishment of process measurements should not be viewed as a tool to be used to build a case for disciplining employees or for justifying merit raises. Effective process measures must provide top management the feedback they need to ensure that the incredibly complex symphony that is your organization plays on.

SUMMARY

- Top management needs data and information to make effective decisions.

- Many public-sector organizations use performance measures to defend performance rather than improve it.

- It's not important to have hundreds of measures; it's important that the organization develops measurements that support the achievement of the organization's overall quality objectives.

- All processes are required to be monitored and/or measured. Methods for monitoring/measurement of processes must demonstrate the ability of the processes to achieve desired results.

- The organization must develop appropriate methods for monitoring/ measurement of products or services against requirements.

- Measures and other data must be collected and analyzed to identify where improvement of the quality management system can be made.

- Shewhart control charts and Pareto analysis are excellent tools for analysis of data.

- People are not hired to do a job; they are hired to accomplish an objective.

- Once process objectives are defined, measurements should be developed that provide data and information that can be used to determine if the process objectives are being achieved.

- An anecdotal approach to management promotes the establishment of kingdoms and fiefdoms in public-sector organizations as individual divisions or offices learn to wage war on each other in the fight for resources.

- A measurement system that is well integrated with the organization's overall objectives and goals will provide the facts and data that top management needs to allocate resources based on need and to identify opportunities for improvement.

- No metrics are perfect. The development of a measurement system should be focused on providing data and information to top management that will allow them to make effective decisions when allocating scarce resources.

13

Mutually Beneficial Supplier Relationships

Therefore let our alliance be combined,
Our best friends made, our meinies stretched,
And let us presently go sit in council
How covert matters may be best disclosed,
And open perils surest answered.

—William Shakespeare,
The Tragedy of Julius Caesar

INTRODUCTION

In the eighth year of Julius Caesar's nine-year invasion of Gaul, his Roman army encountered the well-defended, seemingly impenetrable fortress of Alesia. The fort was built upon a one-mile long by one-half-mile wide, oval-shaped plateau that rose 500 feet above the surrounding valley floor. Near the top of the mount, the moderate slopes of the plateau transformed into steep and jagged walls of solid rock. Standing in defiance on the top of this ancient stronghold were 80,000 Gallic warriors. The Roman army numbered no more than 75,000. Instead of sending his men to certain death, Caesar ordered the construction of dual walls surrounding the plateau. The innermost wall was designed to keep the Gallic forces within Alesia from attacking. The outermost wall was designed to block food, supplies, and reinforcements from reaching the fort.

The siege lasted for several months as the Gallic forces within Alesia slowly ran out of food and hope. Caesar's well-engineered blockade kept reinforcements and supplies from reaching Alesia. After a last desperate attempt to break through the cordon, the Gallic leader Vercingetorix surrendered to Caesar's forces. Caesar had engineered the destruction of a critical Gallic garrison and by doing so ensured his eventual success in the conquest of Gaul. Julius Caesar is certainly not the best example of a

117

compassionate leader. After the victory of Uxellodunum he had the hands cut off of all who had borne arms against his army and set them free so that everyone in Gaul could see the punishment that was meted out to those who resisted his army. To say he had a dark side is putting it mildly. Despite his shortcomings in compassion and humility, Caesar was a brilliant military strategist and he clearly understood the symbiotic relationship between an army and its suppliers. One can not exist without the other.

The same concept applies to all organizations. The quality of the products and services provided by private and public companies alike is only as good as the quality of the products and services provided by their suppliers. When it comes to your suppliers, their quality is your quality. An organization is no different from the ancient army of Alesia; it can not exist without its suppliers.

MEETING THE UNIQUE CHALLENGES OF PUBLIC-SECTOR ORGANIZATIONS

It's an interesting phenomenon that many of the legislative representatives who run for office on a platform of making government agencies operate more like private businesses create laws that prohibit the achievement of their desired objective. Nowhere is this paradox more troubling than in the area of procurement. One of W. Edwards Deming's famous 14 points for management was to end the practice of awarding business solely on the basis of price tag. Deming believed that organizations should work to reduce the number of suppliers for the same item, reasoning that a higher number of suppliers would result in a higher level of variation. This stands in stark contrast to the goal of many public-sector organizations to increase the number of suppliers. How can this dichotomy between the interest of public agencies and the fundamentals of quality management be reconciled?

The answer lies in integrating the supply chain into your quality management system. Measures of performance and analysis of nonconformities need to be communicated to each supplier so that they can make changes to their own system to improve their ability to meet your organization's requirements. Just as PDCA is critical to the continual improvement of your organization, the implementation of this principle must be planned, designed, and implemented for your supply chain. See Figure 13.1.

Over the years, the emphasis on ensuring that requirements have been met by suppliers has given rise to an overemphasis on simply ensuring that specifications are met. From this perspective, quality means that requirements have been met. In the context of the ISO 9001 standard, quality

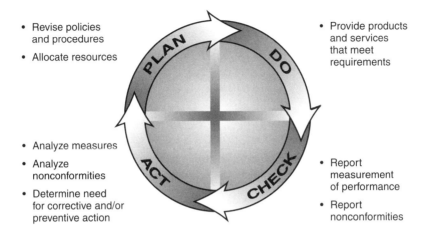

- Revise policies and procedures
- Allocate resources

- Provide products and services that meet requirements

- Analyze measures
- Analyze nonconformities
- Determine need for corrective and/or preventive action

- Report measurement of performance
- Report nonconformities

Figure 13.1   Supplier PDCA.

is defined as the degree to which a set of inherent characteristics fulfills requirements. In other words, quality doesn't mean simply meeting the specification. Quality means the degree to which the finished product fulfills the requirements of the specification. Quality begins at conformance and increases as variation is removed. The importance of this paradigm in our relationship with our suppliers can not be overstated. Instead of policing our suppliers to ensure they meet the minimum specifications, we must work with them to improve their ability to meet our requirements. To accomplish this formidable task, we must apply many of the same concepts of management review, monitoring and measurement, and corrective and preventive action to our suppliers. One of Deming's famous principles for transformation of American industry concerns the removal of barriers that rob people of their pride of workmanship. The same principle applies to our suppliers. Applying the principles of ISO 9001 to our supply chain gives pride of workmanship back to our suppliers.

CLAUSE 7.4.1: PURCHASING PROCESS

Clause 7.4.1 of the ISO 9001 standard requires the organization to evaluate and select suppliers based on their ability to supply products or services in accordance with the organization's requirements. At IDOT, this was definitely one area where we were already meeting the minimum requirements of the standard. Over the course of many years, controls on procurement

Table 13.1 Examples of IDOT controls on suppliers.

Supplier	Method of evaluation and selection	Controls	Performance measures
Construction contractors	• Competitive sealed bidding • Low bid	• Prequalification • Oversight by award committee	• Evaluations of contractor performance • Financial ratings
Engineering consultants	• Firms submit statements of interest • Competitive evaluation of professional and technical qualifications	• Prequalification • Award made by selection committee	• Evaluations of consultant performance • Financial ratings
General supplies and services	• Request for proposals (RFPs) • Competitive sealed bidding	• Statement of qualification reviewed against RFP requirements by chief procurement officer	• Post-performance review • Formal process for reporting vendor noncompliance

of construction contracting services, engineering consulting services, and commodities have been established in a complex framework of state and federal statutory and regulatory requirements. Sophisticated systems have been developed to support the achievement of these requirements and to aid in the identification of opportunities for improvement and the communication of performance to our suppliers. Table 13.1 provides the methods of evaluation and selection, unique controls, and method of measuring performance employed at IDOT for each type of supplier.

CLAUSE 7.4.2: PURCHASING INFORMATION

Clause 7.4.2 of the ISO 9001 standard requires that the following requirements be incorporated into purchasing information as appropriate:

1. Requirements for approval of product, procedures, processes, and equipment

2. Requirements for qualification of personnel

3. Quality management system requirements

All this really means is that the organization must specify what it wants to purchase in a defined and detailed manner. At IDOT, most of these requirements are documented or at least referenced in our contracts. Each contract specifies the requirements the vendor must meet. For a typical construction contract, we may specify that a certain piece of equipment must be used. For an engineering contract, we may specify that all structural work must be reviewed and approved by a licensed structural engineer. In all contracts, we specify how unacceptable work (or work that does not meet requirements) is dealt with and what corrective and preventive action is required to be implemented by the supplier.

CLAUSE 7.4.3: VERIFICATION OF PURCHASED PRODUCT

Clause 7.4.3 of the ISO 9001 standard requires the organization to establish and implement the inspection or other activities necessary for ensuring that purchased product meets specified purchase requirements. Where verification is intended to be conducted at the supplier's premises, the organization is required to state the intended arrangements and method of release in the purchasing information. Table 13.2 provides a summary of the different kinds of verification activities employed at IDOT.

Table 13.2 Examples of IDOT verification requirements.

Supplier	Verification activity
Construction contractor	Material and construction inspection and documentation
Engineering consultant	Review of engineering documents produced against requirements of policies and procedures
General supplies and services	Signature is required on invoices certifying that supplies or services were received in accordance with contract specifications

ISO 9001 CERTIFICATION OF YOUR SUPPLIERS

The ISO 9001 standard isn't just a quality management system; it's a system for managing a business. Financial measures are critical to the success of any organization and should be an important part of any organization's quality plan. The focus on managing activities as processes leads to increased *internal* service quality. Well-managed internal processes promote higher levels of employee retention and productivity, which lead to effective and efficient operations. Thus, a properly implemented ISO 9001 quality management system that is aligned with the organization's strategic objectives can increase the profitability of the business while increasing customer satisfaction through improved project quality. Incentives can be developed that require suppliers to implement an effective management system like ISO 9001. This approach benefits all stakeholders by improving the efficiency and effectiveness of the organization's processes in a way that doesn't conclude with the completion of a specific project. Continued compliance to the ISO 9001 standard requirements can create further opportunities for improvement and will improve the ability of the organization to meet stakeholder requirements and exceed expectations while improving the profitability of its business.

That being said, demanding ISO 9001 certification of your suppliers could create a tremendous headache for your organization. Besides the tremendous resistance that you will likely encounter from the supply chain, you will also expend considerable resources to educate suppliers in the implementation of the new requirement. A middle-of-the-road approach where the principles of ISO 9001 are adopted in your organization's purchasing process and resulting oversight activities can yield considerable benefits. The same principles of management review, monitoring and measurement, and corrective and preventive action that are used in your own organization can also be applied jointly with your suppliers. By enforcing this type of understanding within your suppliers, you will not only improve the quality of the products and services they provide for your organization, you will help them improve their business and they will thrive. Regardless of the approach your organization adopts, it's important to remember this fundamental principle: when your suppliers succeed, you succeed.

SUMMARY

- An organization and its suppliers are interdependent.

- Misguided procurement legislation has resulted in an overemphasis on conformance instead of quality and continual improvement.

- In order to move beyond compliance toward true quality and continual improvement, public-sector organizations should integrate their supply chain into their quality management system.

- All organizations should work to give pride of workmanship back to their suppliers.

- Suppliers must be evaluated and selected based on their ability to supply product in accordance with the organization's requirements.

- Purchasing requirements must be defined.

- The organization must establish and implement the necessary processes for ensuring that purchased products meet the organization's requirements.

- Incorporating ISO 9001 requirements into your supply chain will help your suppliers improve their operations and become more productive and efficient. This will improve profitability for them while increasing their ability to meet requirements.

14

Putting It All Together

*It sounded an excellent plan, no doubt, and very neatly
and simply arranged; the only difficulty was, that she
had not the smallest idea how to set about it.*

—Lewis Carroll, *Alice's Adventures in Wonderland*

INTRODUCTION

For the majority of this book, I have tried to present to you the intent of the ISO 9001 standard requirements by viewing the requirements through the lens of the eight quality management principles. In order to demonstrate the correct application of these requirements, I have used many examples of my experiences at the Illinois Department of Transportation. Managing an organizational approach to quality management like ISO 9001 is a daunting task. Many of the techniques we used in the beginning of our certification effort didn't work. Finding the right approach for our organization was at times a confusing voyage filled with lots of trial and error.

In writing this book, my original plan was to simply explain to you our journey through this iterative process and encourage you to develop your own strategy. As I pondered this approach, I remembered my own frustrations with finding any guidance whatsoever on how to manage an ISO 9001 certification effort. Most of the articles I read were rather abstract and provided some simple concepts for managing the effort but supplied precious little practical advice. In retrospect, I now understand that managing our certification program was a valuable learning experience, and had we used a cookie cutter process, we wouldn't have learned nearly as much about the organization as we did. It would be disingenuous for me to claim that I can provide you with a bulletproof method for implementing and managing an ISO 9001 certification program in your organization. What I can offer you are some overarching concepts and building blocks for you to construct your own plan of attack.

In this chapter, I will provide you with an approach that is a combination of actual strategies employed by IDOT and some best practices discovered through the rectification of many mistakes. It is a simple plan of action that can be implemented in any organization regardless of the number of employees or the geographical proximity of the organizational components. It is important that you understand that this approach should only be used as a guide in the development of your own strategy. This blueprint must be carefully tailored to meet the specific goals and objectives of your certification program and aligned with your organization's unique culture and strengths.

Okay, enough with the disclaimer. Let's get started.

FIRST THINGS FIRST

Take a deep breath and relax. I can almost guarantee that you are already more than halfway toward your goal of conformance to the ISO 9001 standard before you even get started. Many of the requirements of the standard are simply good business practices, and it is very likely that your organization has already implemented policies and procedures that address some of those requirements. Creation of an ISO 9001–based management system is certainly a difficult task but it's not insurmountable by any means. You *can* do it and you *will* do it if you take the time to develop a strategic approach to the implementation of the ISO 9001 standard in your organization.

Take some time to determine the objectives of the ISO 9001 program. Why are you pursuing certification? Is speed of the essence? You can get certified fast or you can get certified right but you can't do both at the same time. Depending on the culture of your organization and political realities, you'll likely take one path or the other. If ISO 9001 certification is being pursued in response to a major public relations fiasco within the organization, speed will probably be your primary objective. If ISO 9001 certification is being pursued to bring needed change to an organization that is hopelessly stuck in the past, a more deliberate course is probably advisable. The objectives of the program will guide the development of the proper strategy you'll need to adopt in order to achieve your goals.

Once you've developed objectives for the program and you can define success, it's recommended that you employ a strategic approach. Let's take a pragmatic approach for just a few moments and identify the high-level steps that must be accomplished before the registrar arrives to determine the level of conformance within the organization to the requirements of the ISO 9001 standard. The most important task to be completed is a gap analysis. In Chapter 10, we discussed a method for completing a gap analysis using your own staff. If resources are not available within the organization to conduct this analysis, there are plenty of consultants who will gladly charge you several thousand dollars for this exercise. If you choose to outsource this activity, *do not* allow the consultant to interview staff unaccompanied at any time or a tremendous amount of information will walk out the door with the consultant when the gap analysis is completed. Another thing to remember is that most consultants will not possess sufficient knowledge of your organization's policies and procedures to hit the ground running. A consultant in your organization is like a new employee. Without assistance, she will likely face a long learning curve as she struggles to understand the peculiarities of your organization. A guide should be with the consultant at all times to aid in the translation between the language of the standard and the unique culture of your organization. At IDOT, our consultant told us we had a major problem because we did not have adequate controls for our forms. He cited clause 4.2.3 of the standard and suggested that we use a numbering convention that tied in directly with the numerical clauses of the ISO 9001 standard. This predictable knee-jerk response ended up costing us countless hours of lost productivity as we scrambled to add ISO numbers to all of our forms (today we have more than 1000!). Fortunately for us, before we got too far along with the conversion of each and every business form, a career employee quietly pointed out to us that while we didn't utilize an ISO clause numbering convention, we *did* have unique identifiers for all of our forms. The form of control we utilized for our forms may not have been what our consultant was used to seeing, but it *did* meet the requirements of the ISO 9001 standard.

Once the gap analysis is completed and you have adequately identified the areas of the organization's policies and procedures that do not conform to the requirements of the ISO 9001 standard, you'll need to identify which documents need to be revised and begin work implementing the requirements of the standard in your organization's documentation. When the system has been documented, an internal audit of the entire system must be completed. The results of the audit need to be an input into a management review that should immediately follow the audit. During the management review, the results of the audit, along with process and product measurements, need to be analyzed to determine the need for corrective and preventive actions. Identified action plans resulting from the management review need to be assigned and implemented. Once that's done, it's time to call in the registrar because you're ready for your on-site readiness review. Figure 14.1 provides an overview of this process.

It's been said many times that the first step is always the longest. This cliché is definitely appropriate to an ISO 9001 certification program.

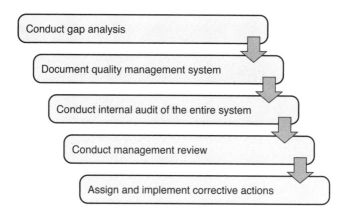

Figure 14.1 The march to certification.

Managing an initiative that impacts the entire organization can seem mind-boggling in the beginning. Where do we start? How do we begin? To borrow from another cliché, one tackles this task the same way one eats an entire elephant: one bite at a time. It may not be easy but it is *simple*.

CONDUCT A FORCE FIELD ANALYSIS

Implementing an ISO 9001 certification program can be difficult because it represents a radical departure from the status quo. In order to develop an effective strategy to manage this change, it is recommended you complete a force field analysis. A force field analysis is a simple tool that allows you to anticipate the forces that will resist or support a change initiative. It's a very simple exercise that culminates in the production of a list of different forces within the organization and an assessment of whether each force will resist or support the change initiative. Completing this exercise will help you identify an effective strategy for managing the organizational change necessary to implement the ISO 9001 standard within your organization. This strategy will allow you to mitigate the forces that could hold back progress while simultaneously identifying ways to build momentum for the certification program by using any element of the organization that will support the ISO 9001 certification program. An example of a force field analysis is shown in Figure 14.2.

The force field analysis should be the first step in a much larger strategy for effective implementation of the ISO 9001 standard requirements.

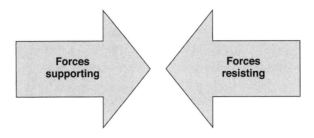

ISO 9001 certification	
Forces supporting	**Forces resisting**
Stakeholders (legislature, public) want change	Little room in operating budget for ISO training
Director is informed and supportive of ISO 9001 certification	Mid-level managers not well informed of quality management basics or ISO 9001 benefits
Current system is well documented in manuals and operating procedures	Control of forms and templates is very spotty. All areas control distribution of forms differently.

Figure 14.2   Force field analysis example.

By conducting a field force analysis to identify the forces supporting and resisting ISO 9001 certification in your organization, you can construct a more effective strategy for implementation.

MANAGING THE CERTIFICATION EFFORT

Once you have completed your force field analysis, it's time to figure out how you will manage the overall program. I found that the key to success in getting a quality management system up and running in our organization was to focus on five critical elements of the standard: document/record control, internal audit, management review, corrective and preventive actions, and the organization's measurement system. If you wish to follow a similar approach, the creation of a steering committee to review the results of the gap analysis, identify team members to review the ISO 9001 requirements for each critical element, and to provide guidance for the overall program is advisable. The ISO 9001 standard clearly identifies the requirements that must be met for each of these critical elements so there is little need for the steering committee to take a hands-on approach to managing these teams. Identify the leaders and team members with the drive and competency to complete the task, give them a goal and some boundaries, and get out of their way. Figure 14.3 shows an example of a strategy.

The ISO 9001 steering committee should be formally chartered, with rules and responsibilities clearly stated along with objectives and expectations.

In order to ensure that all employees feel like they are involved in the ISO 9001 program, it is advisable to develop a simple communication plan. This plan does not need to be elaborate, nor exciting and flashy. Elegance should always be a major goal of internal communication: delivering the message to the recipient in the simplest, most cost-effective manner possible. It is for this reason that I have not included a communication team as part of the ISO 9001 steering committee. Communication regarding the ISO 9001 certification program should be incorporated into your existing internal communication processes. Like all other processes of the quality management system, communication must have measurable objectives identified so that analysis can be performed to identify opportunities for improvement. Table 14.1 contains an example of a simple communication plan for disbursing information about an ISO 9001 certification program to employees.

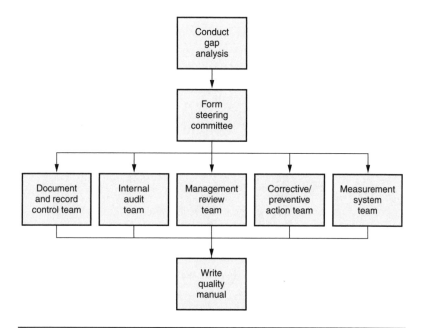

Figure 14.3   Example strategy for ISO 9001 certification.

Table 14.1 Example communication plan.

Frequency	Communication
Weekly	E-mail from ISO management representative explaining progress made during the previous week
Monthly	Meeting with steering committee to review progress made during the previous month and to identify any roadblocks encountered
Quarterly	Newsletter containing important news and informative articles regarding the certification program
Annually	Webinar for all employees to review measures for previous year and objectives for the next year
Continuous	• Post records of management reviews, internal and external audits, and corrective/preventive actions on intranet site for access by all employees • Calendar with important dates identified (for example, internal audit dates, external audit dates, and management review meeting dates) • Intranet site with answers to frequently asked questions, links to ISO's Web site (www.iso.org) and the American Society for Quality (www.asq.org), and a listing for the members of the ISO 9001 steering committee, ISO management representative, and other ISO team members

The key to effective communication is to make it part of your organizational culture. Whatever communication processes you decide to employ should align well with the preferences and limitations of your employees. In other words, if the majority of your employees do not have Internet access, then you should not rely on your organization's intranet page to announce important information regarding the ISO 9001 certification program. Tailor your communication approaches accordingly to create a simple plan for communicating with your employees and stick to it. Nothing will derail an improvement initiative faster than poor communication processes.

IMPORTANT COMPETENCIES YOU'LL NEED

In Chapter 8 we discussed the requirements of clause 6.2.2 of the ISO 9001 standard. The organization is required to determine the competencies of personnel performing work affecting quality. This includes personnel engaged in the construction and maintenance of the quality management

Table 14.2   Example training plan.

Group	Required competencies	Recommended actions
ISO management representative	In-depth understanding of the ISO 9001 standard and the basics of quality management and: • Chair management review meeting • Champion and manage quality improvement initiatives • Communicate the importance of meeting customer requirements throughout the organization	Three- to five-day training course to review ISO 9001 requirements and provide guidance for implementing and auditing an ISO 9001 quality system
Document/records control coordinator	Understanding of ISO 9001 requirements for document control and control of records	One- to two-day training course to review ISO 9001 requirements for document control and control of records
Audit coordinator	Understanding of ISO 9001 requirements for internal audit: • Scheduling, coordination, and implementation of effective internal audits • Verifying the effectiveness of corrective and preventive actions	Five-day RABQSA-certified lead auditor training session
Corrective/ preventive action coordinator	Extensive understanding of root cause analysis and the organization's corrective and preventive action procedures	One-day training session to review the basics of root cause analysis and the ISO 9001 requirements for corrective/preventive action

Continued

Table 14.2 *Continued.*

Group	Required competencies	Recommended actions
Senior management	General understanding of ISO 9001 standard	One-day training session to review ISO 9001 requirements with emphasis on clause 5.0 requirements
Supervisors and process owners	Specific quality management system requirements: • How to initiate corrective or preventive action • Root cause analysis • How to establish process objectives and measures • How to analyze process metrics	One- to two-day training session to review quality system requirements and procedures
All employees	General quality management system requirements: • How to control nonconforming work • What records must be kept, where they are to be stored, and for how long • How to access quality management system documentation • The organization's quality objectives and how their individual activities contribute to their achievement	• Annual webinar or meeting to review status of the organization's quality objectives • New employee orientation • Checklist to be used for on-the-job training by supervisor

system. Table 14.2 provides an example of a training plan to build the necessary competencies that will be needed to build a quality management system.

All of these competencies can be brought in by hiring quality professionals or developed internally by teaching these concepts to employees and requiring them to serve as trainers for other employees. ASQ (www.asq.org) offers many different resources for training, from books and virtual training tools for all employees to intense, week-long courses aimed at building specific competencies such as ISO 9001 lead auditing.

By taking a strategic approach to managing the ISO 9001 certification effort, you will ensure that the basic components of the management system are in place. The framework you will have created will be self-sustaining as the processes that were developed will begin to drive conformance of the system to requirements. Once the effort is rolling along, you will be able to tweak individual components as you move forward.

SUMMARY

- Adopting a strategic approach to implement the ISO 9001 standard within your organization will keep the effort from stalling and will provide the necessary momentum to initiate change.

- Begin with a gap analysis and use your staff to accomplish it if at all possible. If this is not possible, insist that the consultant you hire be accompanied by one of your employees at all times during the analysis to ensure that the information does not walk out the door with the consultant when the analysis is completed.

- Conduct a force field analysis to identify the different forces within the organization that will support or resist the ISO 9001 certification program. Use this information to tailor an approach that will augment the forces supporting the effort while minimizing the impact of the resisting forces.

- Create a formally chartered steering committee to oversee and manage the effort.

- Focus the initial effort on the areas of document/record control, internal audit, management review, corrective/preventive action, and measurement system.

- Create a simple communication plan to keep employees informed about the progress of the ISO 9001 certification effort and stick with it. Nothing will derail an organizational improvement effort faster than poor communication.

- Create a plan to build the specialized competencies you'll need to implement the ISO 9001 standard within your organization, and don't forget about the excellent resources offered by ASQ.

15

The Registrar

Pleased to meet you
Hope you guess my name
But what's puzzling you
Is the nature of my game

—The Rolling Stones, "Sympathy for the Devil"

The most common questions I receive about IDOT's ISO 9001 certification program involve the certification/surveillance audits: "What is the registrar like?" "What are the certification audits like?" "What areas does the registrar review?" These questions don't surprise me because we were asking ourselves the very same questions when we first began this odyssey. I believe the easiest way to answer these types of questions is to describe a typical certification audit from our experience.

First, some clarification is necessary. The registrar is not a person but rather the *organization* that provides certification services. The *auditor* is an agent of the registrar who visits the petitioning organization to determine their level of conformance to the standard. Technically speaking, the auditor can only make a recommendation for certification. Another body—generally a board within the organization—makes the final determination. The terms *registrar* and *auditor* are often used interchangeably, but this is incorrect.

Our registrar is NSF International (NSF) and our current auditor is Kishor Desai. Kishor is a friendly gentleman from Ontario, Canada, with a fierce passion for quality management. He is easygoing and of good humor until the subject turns to quality management. When that happens, his eyes begin to blaze and his speech becomes rushed, almost as if the words come to his mind faster than his ability to communicate them. He is a man with a mission: to generate audit findings that will help the organizations he serves improve their ability to meet the requirements of their customers and exceed their expectations.

Kishor has a unique way of speaking that reminds me of Yoda from the *Star Wars* movies. He often answers a question with another question, and sometimes the structure of his sentences seems a little backwards. As an auditor, Kishor is not allowed to consult, and he is almost religious in his adherence to this mantra. He will sometimes offer questions about certain processes or activities but he leaves the conclusion to us. What has emerged from our collaboration is a true partnership that has benefited both organizations.

This section deals with a surveillance audit that occurred July 28, 2008, through July 31, 2008. Two months prior to the audit, Kishor contacted me, and we discussed the scope of the scheduled audit. The scope of the audit is usually negotiated with the following criteria in mind:

1. Kishor needs to audit the management review, corrective/ preventive action, and internal audit processes during every visit.

2. All processes within the quality management system must be audited at least once during the three-year surveillance period.

3. Processes that involve the customer or that are close to the final product must be audited more frequently.

4. Process audits are most effective when there is actually work being performed. Seasonal processes should be scheduled for audits when they are active.

5. If an audit trail develops during the audit, Kishor must be allowed to deviate from the negotiated scope to close out the trail.

The scope and schedule we negotiated is available as Appendix C. In order to prepare for the audit, I provided electronic copies of our quality documentation to Kishor prior to his visit. I also assembled hard copies of our quality documentation at our facility for his use during the audit. This lead work generally helps facilitate a more effective audit.

OPENING MEETING

The audit began with an opening meeting. The purpose of the opening meeting is twofold:

1. To introduce the auditor to top management

2. To explain the scope of the audit and the standard to which the organization will be audited

Some auditors are very formal and use a checklist of items to review during the opening meeting. Kishor's approach is more instinctual and he generally prefers an open discourse. During the discourse, Kishor weaves the necessary information into the meeting as the subjects and issues come up. I believe this to be a superior way to accomplish the meeting objectives because it keeps the meeting conversational and relaxed. This particular meeting lasted less than 30 minutes, and everyone in attendance was in good spirits when it concluded. When the opening meeting ended, the audit began.

MANAGEMENT REVIEW, CORRECTIVE AND PREVENTIVE ACTION, AND INTERNAL AUDIT PROCESSES

These are the big processes for us. Kishor audits these processes every single visit. I like to think of these three processes as our vital signs. If everything looks good with these activities, the "health" of the quality management system is fairly good and the rest of the audit should go fairly smoothly. If something catches Kishor's eye as he reviews our "vital signs," chances are good he'll be taking a more critical approach when he audits the remainder of the organization and we'll see more findings.

Management review was a fairly simple audit. Kishor reviewed our records (meeting minutes) and compared them to the required inputs and outputs of clause 5.6 of the standard. Follow-up questions are common, and Kishor asked a few during this particular audit:

- Will you please tell me about a corrective or preventive action that was initiated as a result of a management review?

- How do you know your management review process is effective?

- What types of improvements have you been able to implement as a result of your management review process?

- Will you please show me an example where you used the management review process to allocate resources?

- What types of measures do you bring into your management reviews?

- What types of customer feedback do you bring into your management reviews?

The internal audit process was a little more intense due to the nature of the process. A documented procedure is required by the standard, so Kishor had to review our procedure to confirm that it met the requirements of the standard. Kishor then reviewed our internal audit records and confirmed that we are following the requirements of our own procedure. Kishor did this by reviewing the records to ensure that the scope identified in our internal audit plan was achieved and that the appropriate requirements of the standard were verified by the internal auditor with objective evidence.

There were many different requirements to check and not enough time available during the surveillance audit, so Kishor took a small sample by randomly selecting a half dozen internal audit records and closely examined those records against the criteria we had outlined in our internal audit procedure and our internal audit plan. Kishor spot-checked other records by ensuring that the basics like measurable objectives, document and record control, quality policy, and analysis of data had been verified by the internal auditor. At the conclusion of the audit, Kishor checked to ensure that measurable objectives had been established for the internal audit process, and then we discussed the current status of the process.

The corrective/preventive action audit was the simplest audit to accomplish. Kishor selected several completed corrective/preventive actions from our file and reviewed each one to ensure the following:

1. The cause of the nonconformity or potential nonconformity was identified.

2. The proposed corrective or preventive action plan was properly implemented.

3. The implemented corrective or preventive action plan was effective in eliminating the cause of the nonconformity or potential nonconformity.

At IDOT, we created a corrective action request form and a preventive action request form to serve as the primary documents to record any issues identified, the root cause investigation results, the approved corrective or preventive action plan, and the results of the verification activities. Examples of corrective and preventive action request forms are available in Appendix D.

Verifying the effectiveness of the corrective/preventive action process is easy because it's a simple matter to review a fix applied and determine the effectiveness of the actions taken. In other words, the fix applied either worked or it didn't work at all. During this audit, Kishor reviewed the corrective/preventive action record and simply asked me, "Can you show me evidence that this action was implemented?" One corrective action required a change to a procedure, so I showed him the revised procedure. A preventive action required the completion of training for specific personnel, so I showed him the training record. Effectiveness of the implemented corrective/preventive action was confirmed by a review of recent process measures and by a review of nonconformance records.

CONCRETE LABORATORY

The concrete testing laboratory was next on our agenda. Kishor began by asking the concrete laboratory supervisor, "How is the process defined?" Testing procedures were produced, and Kishor immediately checked to determine if the documents were being properly controlled. He then perused the procedure and highlighted several steps seemingly at random. He then sampled several records and confirmed that the highlighted steps were performed. Control of records was reviewed continuously by asking questions such as "Where are the records kept?" "How long do you keep these records?" and "Who is responsible for maintaining these records?"

Kishor then did a quick walk-through of the laboratory. He checked several testing samples to ensure they were properly identified. He checked several pieces of testing equipment to ensure they had been calibrated in accordance with documented procedures. He reviewed the work environment to ensure that equipment had been properly maintained and that testing was being completed under controlled conditions (work instructions are readily available and current, samples are properly identified, and measuring devices are properly calibrated).

Kishor asked the concrete laboratory supervisor about the status of his measurable objectives. The supervisor produced the latest process measures reports, which showed that quality targets had been missed in each of the past two reporting periods. Kishor inquired what actions had been taken as a result of the nonconforming measures reports, and the supervisor told Kishor that no action had been taken. Kishor wrote a nonconformance against clause 8.2.3 of the standard, which states, "When planned results are not achieved, correction and corrective action shall be taken, as appropriate, to ensure conformity of the product." After answering a few questions from the staff of the concrete laboratory, we were off to our next scheduled audit interview.

CONSTRUCTION JOB SITE

We drove out to a construction job site. The job site was a bridge replacement on a rural, two-lane highway about 45 minutes north of the city of

Springfield. Kishor insisted on visiting a project site during this audit so that he could see firsthand the scope of work and talk informally to a few of the construction inspectors. Work was being performed when we arrived, so Kishor checked a few items to ensure conformance with plan and specification requirements. A quick review of the records of concrete strength tests revealed that several tests had not been completed within the time frame required by our procedures. Kishor quickly documented an audit finding to capture the nonconformity and moved on.

Kishor then noticed some reinforcement bars stored on the job site and asked the project manager to furnish the requirements for preservation and identification of product. The project manager produced the contract plans and specifications, and Kishor carefully reviewed them to ensure that the reinforcement bars were properly identified and stored in accordance with the requirements of the specifications. Since the plans and specifications were now in his hand, Kishor used the opportunity to confirm that the distribution of both documents was properly controlled. Kishor then identified the suppliers of several materials that had already been incorporated into the project.

We left the job site and headed straight to the materials office where Kishor produced the list of suppliers he had compiled at the job site. The Materials staff dug through their files and quickly produced copies of material certifications and approved lists. Kishor confirmed that the certifications matched and that all materials sampled were received from approved suppliers.

CLOSING MEETING

The audit concluded with a closing meeting. The purpose of the closing meeting is to review the findings of the audit with the organization's management team and discuss any necessary follow-up. If there are disagreements with the audit findings, these conflicts are discussed and resolved during this meeting. If resolution can not be reached during the closing meeting, there are procedures in place for appealing audit findings.

Kishor announced that the audit was a success and that he would recommend continued certification for IDOT. Kishor explained that he documented five minor nonconformities and three opportunities for improvement during this particular audit. Kishor reviewed each audit finding to ensure there were no misunderstandings. He then identified some areas of concern that he observed during the audit. Kishor believed that management at IDOT should monitor these areas and consider taking action to address them. After a short discussion, Kishor opened the meeting up to questions.

There were several questions regarding follow-up, and Kishor explained that corrective actions were required for the five nonconformities and that follow-up was not mandatory for the opportunities for improvement. After all of the questions were answered, the meeting was adjourned and the audit was complete.

FOLLOW-UP

About a week after the audit concluded, Kishor sent me the final audit report and the audit findings. He informed me that we had 30 days to investigate each nonconformance and develop a proposed corrective action plan. Our certification agreement with NSF requires that all corrective action plans be approved by the auditor no later than 30 days after the date of the final report. We used our corrective action procedure to assign the audit findings for investigation to management in the affected areas. Once we reached agreement on a proposed corrective action plan, we sent the proposed corrective action plan to Kishor for his review. Kishor reviewed the corrective action plans to determine if each one met the requirements of our certification agreement. As part of our certification agreement, we are required to follow a five-step process in addressing registration or surveillance audit findings, as shown in Figure 15.1.

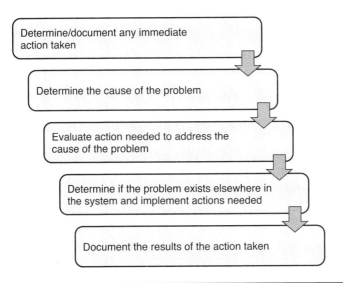

Figure 15.1   Five-step process for addressing external audit findings.

Kishor approved our audit findings and notified us that he would be reviewing each action to verify implementation and effectiveness during the next surveillance audit.

SELECTING A REGISTRAR

The registration industry is fairly competitive. In the United States alone, there are more than 50 ISO 9001 registration organizations and more than 27,000 ISO 9001:2000 certificates. Because of significant competition, substantial cost differences are rare between registration organizations. This allows you to concentrate your attention on identifying a registration organization that best suits the unique requirements of your organization. It's very important to remember that a registrar is simply another supplier for your organization. The ISO 9001 standard requires your organization to evaluate and select suppliers based on their ability to supply product (or service) in accordance with your organization's requirements. Take some time and determine the type of registrar you want for your organization. Find a registrar that has verifiable experience in your field or industry. Ask for references and scrutinize them. Apply the same amount of scrutiny to your selection of a registrar as you would to any other major supplier. You're looking for a mutually beneficial relationship—a partnership that will help both of your organizations improve. The best registrars have a vested interest in your continued improvement and will hold you accountable to the requirements of the standard for this reason.

The cost of registration depends on the size of your organization and the complexity of operations. Most registration organizations will provide you a quote for the purposes of determining start-up costs. Be sure to inquire about any costs associated with maintenance of your certification.

AUDITS, NONCONFORMITIES, AND REGISTRATION

Nonconformities are common during both the registration and surveillance audits. This is the name of the game for most auditing organizations. Technically speaking, you've hired a registrar to simply assess your organization's level of conformance to the requirements of the ISO 9001 standard, but this is real life, and the auditor will be working with the understanding that she is being paid to generate audit findings. If the auditor you've chosen isn't documenting nonconformities during her visit, find yourself another auditor.

Several random nonconformities generated by the auditor will not prevent certification so long as an appropriate corrective action plan is submitted within the required time period and approved by the auditor. A major nonconformance may necessitate a delay in your certification but only until the corrective action is implemented and verification is completed by the auditor. This may require a separate site visit by the auditor in order to close it out.

THE AUDIT TEAM

The registrar should identify an audit team with experience in your organization's field. While it's extremely difficult to find an audit team that will be a perfect match for your organization, your registrar should be able to locate an audit team that understands the unique challenges of your industry. This is not as difficult as it sounds. For example, while most auditors may not have actually worked in the engineering field, there are plenty who have audited engineering organizations during their careers. If your registrar can't locate someone with experience in your field to audit your organization, find another registrar.

Conflicts between the audited organization and the audit team occasionally occur during audits. When these conflicts occur, it's to the benefit of both organizations for the people involved to be open and cordial with each other and work toward consensus. If there is a clear disagreement between both parties that can not be resolved, there is an appeal process that may be implemented. This alternative should be used sparingly and only when you are convinced that the audit team's interpretation of the standard is incorrect and addressing the audit finding will result in a great expense of time and/or money for your organization. In the United States, the appeal process begins with a written complaint to the registration organization. If the situation is not resolved to your satisfaction, you may file a written complaint with the ANSI–ASQ National Accreditation Board (ANAB). There are three levels of appeal available within ANAB. The ultimate determination will be made by ANAB, and no further appeal process is available. It is rare that a complaint or appeal will need to travel as far as ANAB. Registration organizations have a strong incentive to keep their customers happy and will work with you to reach consensus in most cases of disagreement.

The choice of a registrar is very important. The ISO 9001 standard requires your organization to evaluate and select your suppliers on their ability to meet the requirements of your organization. This includes the selection of your registrar. Take the time to ensure you've selected an organization that will be a true partner and help your organization improve its operations.

SUMMARY

- A registrar is an organization that is approved to provide certification services. The auditor is an agent of the registrar who visits the petitioning organization to determine their level of conformance to the standard.

- The scope of a registration or surveillance audit is generally negotiated with the registrar and/or the auditor.

- Be sure to provide the auditor adequate access to your quality documentation. This will facilitate a more effective audit.

- The auditor generally reviews management review, internal audit, and corrective/preventive action processes at each visit. Most key processes are reviewed every other visit.

- A registrar is a supplier and should be evaluated on their ability to meet your organization's requirements.

- Request quotes from several registration organizations. Request references and check them thoroughly.

- Nonconformities should be expected during a registration audit and should not be feared. Audit nonconformities will usually not prevent or delay certification so long as an approved corrective action plan is implemented within the required time frame.

- The auditor is a human being, not a robot. They have good days and they have bad days just like everyone else. They are not infallible. Don't be afraid to challenge their findings if you feel they are incorrect.

- There is an appeal/complaint process available to all certified organizations. Use it sparingly but do not be afraid to initiate the process if you are unable to come to agreement with the auditor and you believe his or her interpretation of the standard is incorrect.

- The best registrars will hold you accountable to the requirements of the standard. Look for someone who is tough but fair. You're looking for a partnership.

16

A Word About Sustainability

Whoa, oh, mercy, mercy me
Oh, things ain't what they used to be, no, no
Where did all the blues skies go?

—Marvin Gaye, "Mercy, Mercy Me"

INTRODUCTION

In the spring of 2002, 80 percent of the 1200 students graduating from Princeton University signed a "Grad Pledge" that included a promise to "explore and take into account the social and environmental consequences of any job I consider and . . . try to improve these aspects of any organization for which I work." Times have really changed. When I was a kid, my neighbors dumped used motor oil and antifreeze in the back alley, and people who cared about the environment were called hippies or tree huggers. Pollution was certainly an issue but it wasn't seen as the responsibility of individuals or even most companies. Everyone knew that real pollution was caused by big, evil, profit-seeking corporate leaders. In our minds, public-sector organizations existed to protect the public against the despicable actions of these monolithic, soulless corporations. The concept of individual social responsibility didn't occur to most people.

In the new millennium, sustainability and social responsibility can legitimately be identified as customer requirements for all organizations, public or private. Today's consumer is well educated on the environmental and social impacts of their lifestyles. Couples looking for a diamond ring quiz jewelry store managers about their policy on conflict diamonds, curbside recycling programs abound in most communities, and hybrid vehicles have now become status symbols. According to a recent poll by the Gallup organization, 55% of Americans say they have made changes in their life to protect the environment; 28% say they have made major changes. Clearly this is a trend that leaders of public-sector organizations can not afford to ignore.

MELDING SUSTAINABILITY AND QUALITY MANAGEMENT

Why am I discussing sustainability in a book devoted to quality management? Remember that ISO 9001 defines quality as the "degree to which a set of inherent characteristics fulfills requirements." In order to meet customer requirements in the 21st century, all organizations must practice social responsibility and embrace sustainable business practices. To achieve this end, ISO has worked to align their standard for environmental management systems (ISO 14001) with the ISO 9001 standard. Annex A of the ISO 9001 standard contains a matrix that identifies how the different areas of each standard interrelate. Organizations looking to provide a higher level of assurance for their customers can certify their environmental management system in the same manner as their quality management system.

At a more fundamental level, the overall goals of sustainability and social responsibility can be emphasized by incorporating these concepts into appropriate strategic objectives, translating those throughout the organization, and reviewing progress during regularly scheduled management reviews. That's it. There is no magic to the process except the establishment of goals and a stubborn refusal to give up until the goal is achieved. By aligning the latest buzzword (sustainability) with the quality management system, you will help build momentum and acceptance for the overall certification program.

How to start? Focus first on eliminating waste. Elimination of waste is a fundamental concept in quality management. Waste is rampant in most government organizations due to overspecialization. Lean and kaizen are excellent tools that can help you identify and eliminate waste in your organization. Use the management review process to review data and measures and identify opportunities to improve efficiency by eliminating waste. Eliminating waste will help improve productivity while helping to reduce the organization's overall environmental footprint. Make sure that the results of waste elimination efforts are captured and communicated throughout the organization along with quality metrics.

SUSTAINABILITY OBJECTIVES

Once you've achieved success in implementing waste reduction efforts in the organization, you can branch out toward more sophisticated sustainability objectives. The ISO 26000 standard is currently in draft form, but is anticipated to be released in the fall of 2010. It is a voluntary standard that contains guidance on social responsibility. The standard focuses on seven core social responsibilities:

1. The environment

2. Community involvement and development

3. Human rights

4. Labor practices

5. Fair operating practices

6. Consumer issues

7. Organizational governance

The draft version of the standard is available for review on the ISO/TMB/WG Social Responsibility Web site and also ASQ's Web site. When released, the ISO 26000 standard will provide guidance on the establishment of goals and measures to facilitate effective social responsibility practices. It will be a powerful tool to drive social and environmental accountability in many organizations. My advice to you is to get ahead of the curve now by incorporating the concepts of social responsibility and sustainability into your quality management system. The key to successful implementation is the establishment of social and environmental goals and measurements. It's been said many times and it's still true today—what gets measured gets done.

Social responsibility and sustainability are going to continue to be important issues for customers in the years ahead. Organizations that incorporate these concepts into their management systems will reap significant benefits in reduction of wastes, increased employee satisfaction, and improved public perception. When it comes to social responsibility and sustainability, things definitely ain't what they used to be.

SUMMARY

- Social responsibility and sustainability are customer requirements in the 21st century.

- The overall goals of social responsibility and sustainability can be achieved by establishing goals within the framework of an ISO 9001 quality management system.

- Status of social and environmental goals and measurements should be incorporated into the organization's management review process.

- ISO is currently developing a standard that contains guidance for social responsibility within an organization (ISO 26000).

- Incorporate the concepts of social responsibility and sustainability by establishing social and environmental goals and measurements. What gets measured gets done.

17

What I've Learned

*And it ought to be remembered that there is nothing
more difficult to take in hand, more perilous to conduct,
or more uncertain in its success, than to take the lead in
the introduction of a new order of things.*

—Niccolò Machiavelli, *The Prince*

INTRODUCTION

The past four years have been the most exciting and the most frustrating period of my life. When I was promoted to the newly created position of ISO quality assurance officer for the Illinois Department of Transportation, I found myself thrust into unfamiliar and uncertain territory. I have always been driven by goals and deadlines, and in my mind my latest assignment was no different. I viewed certification of our system as just another goal that I needed to complete, and I threw myself into the task of achieving it in record time. As my understanding of quality management systems grew, my goals seemed to grow farther and farther away from me. I often felt like I was wandering in the desert, my throat parched with a burning thirst for achievement. Many times I thought I could see an oasis beckoning just ahead of me and I'd scramble to the lush wellspring. I would dip my hands into the cool, life-giving water only to come up with a handful of dry, hot sand.

Of all the things I've learned these past four years, the most significant is a greater understanding and appreciation of the concept of continual improvement. Growing up in a society that places a heavy emphasis on individual achievement, I developed a linear perception of reality. In other words, I tended to think of life as a series of tasks that need to be completed. Once a task is accomplished, one should move on to the next task, and so on. My assignment as ISO quality assurance officer provided me with a perplexing problem: there seemed to be no end in sight. When I began this job four years ago, I thought only about reaching a goal. Since that time, my thinking has become more circular in orientation. I now find myself striving toward greater and greater levels of quality with no end in sight. Instead of fixating on a singular goal, I now work every day to continually find ways to improve the quality of my activities. It's a much different mindset than what I'm used to but one that has paid big dividends for me in my career these past few years.

What I'm trying to communicate to you is that the establishment of a quality management system isn't a destination in and of itself. As you will soon discover for yourself, it's the beginning of a never-ending journey of continual improvement for your organization. The remainder of this chapter is filled with my thoughts on quality management and leading change in an organization. I don't pretend to be an expert on either issue. I'm just a guy who has made more than his share of mistakes, and I have tried to learn from each and every one of them. There's an old Chinese saying that goes something like this: "If you would know the road ahead, ask someone who has traveled it." I can't tell you the way to go but I can definitely tell you where I've been and what I learned from it.

BE PATIENT—IT JUST TAKES TIME

In 2005 I attended an ISO 9001 lead auditor training class in Elmhurst, Illinois. On the first day of the class, our instructor wrote "quality management system" on the whiteboard and then drew a 1 to 10 scale below the words. He told us that level 10 represented a quality management system that was robust and proactive in identifying potential problems and achieving high levels of customer satisfaction. Level 1 represented a quality management system that was in its infancy, struggling to meet customer requirements, and reactive to problems as they occurred. The instructor then asked each participant where they felt their organization's quality management system fell on the scale. Most of us answered somewhere around 4 to 6 along the scale. The instructor then added the following to the scale: level 10 = 20+ years to achieve, level 5 = 10+ years to achieve, level 1 = two to three years to achieve. He then asked us, "*Now* where do you think your organization's QMS falls on the scale?" Everyone chuckled nervously. His point had been made.

A properly implemented quality management system is tied directly to the organization's mission, vision, and strategic plan. The policies and procedures that are designed into the quality management system are the tools your employees will use to achieve the long-term strategic goals of the organization. These tools take time to develop. The most important thing to remember in the implementation of your quality management system is that certification isn't the end of the effort—it's the beginning. Certification means you've implemented a process for continual improvement of the organization. Once you achieve certification, you must begin to use it. With each audit, each management review, each corrective or preventive action, your management system improves, and so does your ability to meet customer requirements and exceed expectations. Be patient and remember that it just takes time. There is an old cliché that certainly rings true when applied to the establishment of an ISO 9001 quality management system: It's hard by the yard, but a cinch by the inch.

CHANGE THE CULTURE

It is extremely important that you view the establishment of a quality management system as an enhancement of your existing system of governance, rather than a replacement. Each organization has a unique culture and with it comes a built-in resistance to change. The impact of wholesale elimination of policies and procedures that have served an organization well for decades is akin to the impact of deforestation on an ecosystem. Not only will you harm the environment, you will embolden many employees to become the organizational equivalent of tree huggers. Taking action against these "policy huggers" will create martyrs and heroes for the cause of resistance. Before you know it, a surprisingly sophisticated resistance movement will emerge, and your certification program will grind to a halt.

People cling to policies and procedures because they provide a sense of control and identity to an organization. They create a unique organizational culture. Using an ISO 9001 certification program to clear out old policies and procedures will not produce the results you want to achieve. Removing components of an organization's culture destroys its unique identity, an identity that most employees view with a sense of pride. A better strategy is to review and update these documents with the goal of meeting the requirements of the ISO 9001 standard. Don't get hung up on using the terminology of the ISO 9001 standard. For instance, if your organization uses a different term for validation, don't fight it; simply explain the distinction in your quality manual. There is no need to adopt a new language to conform to the requirements of the ISO 9001 standard. By taking this approach, you will slowly weave the requirements of the ISO 9001 standard into your documentation in a way that is nonthreatening and acceptable to most employees. Most people won't even notice that a change has been made. Before you know it, you just may hear the familiar refrain of "That's just the way we do it here" applied to a component of the ISO 9001 quality management system. When you hear those words, you'll know you were successful.

SELL THE BENEFITS AND CELEBRATE WINS

In many ways, an ISO 9001 certification program is really just another product to be developed and marketed within an organization. This is a critical distinction that must be understood and embraced. Using fear to mandate conformance to the procedures and requirements of a quality management system misses the point of the entire exercise. The psychologist Abraham Maslow identified five basic human needs. He postulated that each of these needs build upon each other, and human beings are not able to move toward a higher level of reasoning unless they first feel their basic needs have been met. Figure 17.1 demonstrates Maslow's hierarchy of needs.

Not all psychologists agree with the specifics of Maslow's theory, but the basic premise is indisputable: human beings can not be expected to function at a high level of creativity and innovation if their basic needs have not been met. The importance of addressing these basic needs is critical to successfully managing organizational change. Maslow further postulated that the five human needs were progressive in nature. In other words, human beings can not move to the next higher level of development until lower-level needs are met. So let's say you're getting ready to meet with your employees to kick off an ISO 9001 certification program and you

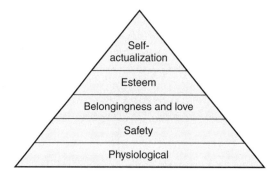

Figure 17.1 Maslow's hierarchy of needs.

want to inspire them to participate and help make it a success. By incorporating Maslow's hierarchy of needs, you can create a simple strategy for your presentation/discussion:

1. *Provide food.* Employees can not be expected to be receptive to your message if they are hungry. Whether or not it is your responsibility to make sure they are fed is irrelevant.

2. *Assure employees that their job is safe.* Many employees see "efficiency" initiatives as nothing more than thinly veiled attempts to eliminate people. Take the time to explain that no one is going to be disciplined or fired because of the program.

3. *Do something to inspire a team mentality.* Instinctively, employees need to belong to a team or group. Use inclusive language in your discussions (we, you). Talk about the company as a family. Incorporate company values and images into the meeting.

4. *Praise their previous efforts.* Use performance measures to demonstrate the skill and hard work of your employees. Explain that the ISO 9001 certification program is meant to *enhance* their efforts.

5. *Give them the facts.* Once you have addressed each of the four basic human needs, employees will now be ready to accept the facts and will be able to better see the potential benefits of the program. Give them an honest assessment of the benefits and don't forget to present the costs of the program.

Once the program is up and rolling, take the time to celebrate wins. This is necessary to maintain momentum and to remind employees of the reasons for the program. Take a cue from society as a whole: people love to celebrate. Here in America we celebrate the birthdays of dead presidents, the anniversaries of important accomplishments, and the beheading of a saint by a Roman emperor in the second century (Valentine's Day). Our celebrations help us establish a unique cultural identity and by doing so they bring us together as a country. The same principle applies to your organization. Logically speaking, celebrations are fruitless and time-consuming. From a practical standpoint, they are absolutely essential to the success of your certification program. Employees need to feel ownership of the quality management system and this can not happen unless your organization celebrates wins together on a regular basis. These celebrations do not need to be lavish: coffee and doughnuts one morning, cake and punch on an afternoon. Plan to celebrate the completion of major steps when you're building the quality management system. then celebrate successful audits once your system is certified. One note of caution—keep remarks to a minimum. The intent is for the team to relax and celebrate an accomplishment. Celebrations are not an opportunity for executives to wow subordinates with an inspiring speech. The management representative should speak for five or 10 minutes or so to set the tone for the celebration by saying, "Here's what we achieved, here's what we'll do next, and thanks to all of you for making this possible."

LEARNED HELPLESSNESS AND THE PSYCHOLOGY OF CONTROL

In her book *The Psychology of Control*, Ellen Langer documented the results of an amazing study of induced disability in nursing home patients. The methodology employed for the study was an experiment involving residents of an intermediate-care facility. The residents were randomly assigned to three groups and given the same 10-piece jigsaw puzzle to complete. Each Group I participant was assigned an examiner who "helped" the resident in locating puzzle pieces. Group II participants were assigned an examiner who simply encouraged them to complete the puzzle but provided no direct assistance. Group III participants received no assistance or encouragement. Subjects in all three groups were given a pretest and a posttest of puzzle assembly performance on their own. The results of the study were astounding. Participants in the "helped" group (group I) not only performed worse on posttests than participants in the "encouraged" group (group II), they performed worse than participants in the "no contact" group (group III). The "encouraged" group (group II) showed the best performance in all categories, but especially so in improvements in speed of performance. The average speed per puzzle piece completed improved 10 times more for the "encouraged" group (17.7 seconds faster) than for the "helped" group (1.8 seconds faster). When the participants of this exercise were asked on the posttest how confident they were that they could successfully complete a similar puzzle in the future, participants in the "helped" group consistently rated their confidence lower than that of the "encouraged" group. The results of the study suggest that a feeling of helplessness is not always grounded in the reality of the situation. Helplessness, it seems, can be learned.

An understanding of the devastating effects of learned helplessness is an important component of any change management initiative. Well-intentioned efforts to help employees complete their tasks or prepare for audits can paradoxically lead to *lower* performance and confidence. As your organization moves forward with the changes to policies and procedures that will be necessary to meet the requirements of the ISO 9001 standard, many employees will seek your assistance. At times like this, it's extremely important that you only provide knowledge and encouragement to these employees. You must resist the urge to do things for them. By helping your employees complete certain activities, you will actually reduce their performance rather than improve it.

In order to perform at a high level, employees need to feel they have some control over their situation. A perception of control and the resulting feeling of ownership it provides is a basic need of optimum human performance. A great way to provide a sense of control and ownership to your employees is to ask them questions. It's been said that average leaders spend their days answering questions while great leaders spend their days *asking* questions. Look to your employees for solutions to the organization's most vexatious problems. When you find a good idea, act on it immediately and let everyone know about the brilliant employee(s) who came up with the idea. Taking this approach will help avoid the phenomenon of "learned helplessness" while providing a much needed sense of control for your employees.

DEVELOP THE LEADERS OF TOMORROW, TODAY

To effect meaningful change in an organization requires a fundamental change in the values of its leadership. Theoretically speaking. this can be accomplished by changing the alignment of the organization's reward system toward the achievement of performance goals that support the initiative in question. This is a fundamental concept of human psychology: behavior that is rewarded is repeated. By changing the focus of the reward system, top management can influence the decisions that are made throughout the organization. It is the aggregate result of these decisions that accomplishes the strategy of the organization much more so than any decisions that are made in the executive conference room.

Human beings do not always behave predictably, and a small segment of employees will resist the proposed changes no matter how well structured the reward system. In most instances, these employees simply will not have the capacity or the will to change their behaviors. The desire to focus your efforts on forcing this group into compliance will be overwhelming and absolutely must be ignored. If you should embark on a vendetta to coerce these employees into submission, two things will likely occur. First of all, you will establish an understanding that poor performance and attitude will receive the lion's share of your efforts and attention. If 80 percent of your efforts are spent bringing your lowest performers in the organization up to an acceptable level of performance, what happens to the rest of the organization? The rest of your employees will quickly feel disengaged from the effort due to your inattention and their performance will fall off. By focusing your efforts on the lowest performers you lower the bar for everyone. Secondly, and most importantly, you will create an environment of fear that will be counterproductive to the goals of the ISO 9001 certification effort.

This should not be construed to suggest that open insubordination should ever be tolerated. Employees must be held to the requirements of their job responsibilities. Individuals who do not complete required responsibilities and authorities must be dealt with in accordance with applicable policies and procedures. The issue at hand is whether or not you are better served spending time with your low performers or your high performers. Time is a limited commodity. Every human being has 24 hours available to him or her in any given day, and you are no exception. When allocating this scarce resource, you absolutely must focus your time and energy on the areas of the organization that will provide you the largest return on your investment. At least 80 percent of your time must be focused on the top performers in your organization. By focusing your efforts on your top performers, you will be developing the leaders of tomorrow. Involve your top performers as often as possible in every aspect of the ISO 9001 certification program. When they move into higher and higher levels of the organization (and they will), they will take with them an understanding and appreciation for the concepts of quality management.

JUST DO IT! DON'T WAIT FOR THE PERFECT TIME TO START

Many public-sector organizations are notorious for avoiding decisions. When contemplating a change initiative such as ISO 9001 certification, executives often initiate an endless string of feasibility studies, exploratory committees, and probationary working groups. While it's advisable to study the issue adequately and gather the facts, there often exists a tremendous temptation to put off the decision until the time is right. Unfortunately, the timing is rarely optimal. There is always a crisis to solve, fires to put out, and things happening that aren't supposed to be happening. The whole point of implementing an ISO 9001 management system in your organization is to help you better manage operations, anticipate and adapt to sudden change, and identify opportunities for improvement. In their bestselling book *The*

Strategy-Focused Organization, Robert Kaplan and David Norton suggest that organizations who fully implemented bad strategy actually performed better over time than those organizations who developed good strategies but failed to implement them effectively. Don't be afraid of making mistakes; you'll make them regardless of whether you start today or two years from now. If you want to implement a quality management system in your organization, do it now. Don't wait for the perfect time to start because that day will never arrive.

Even if the decision is made to implement the ISO 9001 standard within the organization, there will probably be a powerful temptation to "try it out" by only applying the standard in a small portion of the organization. I can sympathize with the reluctance of executives to disrupt the operations of the organization, but the ISO 9001 standard isn't a typical quality management tool. Although approaches like lean and Six Sigma can be successfully implemented piecemeal throughout the organization (although the long-term benefits of these "improvements" are questionable if they did not originate from a thorough assessment and analysis of impact to the overall system), ISO 9001 is an *organization-wide* approach. Trying to implement the requirements of the ISO 9001 standard in one area of the organization is almost guaranteed to create more work for you than if you simply implemented the standard requirements throughout the entire organization. Implementing the requirements throughout the entire organization allows you the freedom to fold your existing policies and procedures into the management system by simply revising these documents to comply with the requirements of the ISO 9001 standard. Implementing the requirements of the ISO 9001 standard in a small area of the organization will result in two layers of controls: one for the "certified" area and one for the rest of operations. Your organization will need to expend a tremendous amount of energy in order to maintain two separate layers of control. More devastatingly, you will have divided the organization into two segments, each with separate goals. When it comes to the implementation of the ISO 9001 standard in your organization, do it all or don't do it at all.

IN CONCLUSION, I'D LIKE TO THANK THE ACADEMY . . .

If there was only one piece of advice I could give you before you set out on your ISO 9001 voyage, it would be this: do everything with integrity. If you say you are going to do something, do it. If you can't do something, then don't promise it. Nothing is more disheartening for employees than a long list of broken promises. If you create a new policy that all employees are expected to observe, make damn sure you follow it to the letter. Human beings are highly sensitive to hypocrisy, and your actions as a leader establish mores for the organization. If you observe the rules, strong mores will develop within the organization because employees will understand that the rules are for everyone. When you make a mistake, own up to it immediately and explain what you are going to do to ensure that it doesn't happen again. Nothing is more pathetic than a leader who refuses to take responsibility. People will tolerate your mistakes if you are open and honest about them but will not tolerate deceit. Always deal with everyone openly and honestly in all of your dealings. Disguising bad news doesn't help anyone. Present the facts as you see them and let the chips fall where they may. Many years ago one of my supervisors told me, "John, the sun shines on everything eventually. You just can't hide the truth forever because it always comes out in the end." Do everything you do with integrity and you need never fear the sun or the truth.

SUMMARY

- The establishment of a quality management system isn't a destination in and of itself; it's the beginning of your journey toward continual improvement.

- A quality management system requires a lot of patience and time to mature. With each audit, with each management review, each corrective or preventive action, your system will improve.

- Don't discard policies and procedures that have served the organization well for decades. Work instead to weave the ISO 9001 requirements into these documents as they are revised.

- An ISO 9001 certification program is really just another product that must be developed and marketed to your employees.

- Remember that human beings can not be expected to function at a high level of creativity and innovation if their basic needs have not been met.

- Once the certification program is up and running, don't forget to take some time to celebrate wins and important milestones.

- Avoid the phenomenon of "learned helplessness." Encourage your employees but resist the urge to do things for them. By helping your employees complete certain activities, you may actually reduce their performance rather than improve it.

- Involve your organization's top performers as often as possible in every aspect of the ISO 9001 certification program. When they move into higher and higher levels of the organization, they will take with them an understanding and appreciation for the concepts of quality management.

- If you want to implement a quality management system in your organization, do it now. Don't be afraid of making mistakes; you'll make them regardless of whether you start today or two years from now.

- When it comes to implementation of the ISO 9001 standard in your organization, do not attempt to implement it piecemeal. Do it all or don't do it at all.

- Do everything with integrity—always.

Well that's it! I hope you have enjoyed reading this book as much as I have enjoyed writing it. If you made it to the end of my quality manifesto then you must surely possess the two most important ingredients of personal success: passion and commitment. Armed with these two attributes, anything is possible; without them, even the most trivial tasks become insurmountable. If you have decided to pursue implementation of the ISO 9001 standard in your organization, I have absolutely no doubt that you will succeed. Be patient, work hard, and most of all, have fun. Remember that's it's not about achieving perfection; it's about continual improvement. As I like to say, the road to success is always under construction.

Appendix A

Example of a Personal Scorecard

ISO Quality Assurance Officer—Measures Report—1st Quarter CY2009					
Objective	**Measurement**	**Target**	**Current status**	**Analysis**	**Follow-up needed**
Use effective internal audits to assure compliance with documented procedures	Number of registrar findings (major nonconformities) not identified first by the internal audit team	≤ 1 per year	0	No major nonconformities recorded this quarter	Continue to monitor
Assure that effective corrective actions are implemented when quality problems are identified	Number of corrective actions found to be not effective as a ratio of total corrective actions documented	8% by January 1, 2010	10.0%	Root cause analysis virtual training session was conducted in January to improve performance	Continue to monitor to determine effectiveness of root cause analysis training session
	Number of preventive actions documented as a ratio of total number of corrective actions documented	15% by January 1, 2010	11.4%	CAR 215 initiated to address performance	Continue to monitor
	Number of audit CARs/total number of CARs documented	10% by January 1, 2010	6.8%	New goal established for CY2009. Implementation of CAR 215 should help improve performance.	Continue to monitor

Continued

Continued

Objective	Measurement	Target	Current status	Analysis	Follow-up needed
	Number of CARs initiated this quarter	N/A	10	January 2009 surveillance audit findings	Continue to monitor
	Number of PARs initiated this quarter	N/A	0	0 preventive actions documented this quarter	Continue to monitor
Effectively communicate departmental quality objectives and assure alignment of individual/ team objectives	Employee survey—mean score of employees' responses to strategic planning category	2.55 (2008 survey results)	2.80 (preliminary numbers)	Preliminary results show improvement Review final report when released to identify target for 2009	Analyze final report when released and develop new target for 2009
Research and evaluate new quality improvement techniques	Quality-related PDHs obtained	15 per year	0	0 PDHs earned this quarter	None
Maintain PE license	Engineering-related PDHs obtained	15 per year	25.5	6 PDHs— 2009 THE conference 19.5 PDHs— 2009 TCM conference	None
Conduct effective management reviews of the performance of the management system	Average score of responses from meeting attendees to the statement "This meeting made good use of my time"	3.0	0	No management reviews conducted this quarter	Next PPC meeting tentatively scheduled for May 2009

Appendix B
Example Internal Audit Forms

**Internal Quality System
Audit Worksheet**

Auditor name:		Date:
Location:	Interviewed:	
Process name:		

INPUTS
What are the inputs to this process?
Where do the inputs come from?
Are they received in a timely manner? ❏ Y ❏ N
If no, explain:
Do the inputs meet the requirements of this process? ❏ Y ❏ N
If no, explain:

OUTPUTS
What is produced by this process?
Who is the customer of this process?
What feedback is received from the customer of this process?
What are the objectives of this process?
What measures have been established to support achievement of the process objectives?

Internal Quality System Audit Worksheet

CONTROLS
Who is responsible for the process and how is this responsibility documented?
How is the process defined?
What statutory and regulatory requirements apply and how are they defined?
What are the customer requirements and how are they defined?
What are the process acceptance criteria and how are they defined?

PROCESS
What are the process steps?
What records are generated?
Review several random samples of records. List the records sampled:
Do the records demonstrate conformance to process requirements? ❏ Y ❏ N
If no, list audit finding number(s):

Internal Quality System Audit Worksheet

RESOURCES
What equipment and resources are required?
Is the equipment suitable and maintained according to requirements? ❏ Y ❏ N
What are the competence requirements?
Is there evidence that people are suitably trained? ❏ Y ❏ N
If yes, list objective evidence:
If no, list audit finding number(s):
Is any measuring and/or monitoring equipment used for this process? ❏ Y ❏ N

If yes, list the measurement and/or monitoring equipment used:

If yes, has the equipment been properly calibrated according to requirements? ❑ Y ❑ N
If no, list audit finding number(s):

EFFECTIVENESS CHECK
Are process measures being collected and analyzed according to plan? ❑ Y ❑ N
What is the current status of process objectives and measures?
When required results are not met, is appropriate action being taken? ❑ Y ❑ N

**Internal Quality System
Auditor Finding**

Audit location:		Audit date:
Auditor initals/finding or observation number	Office/bureau	ISO 9001:2008 element requirement

❏ Major ❏ Minor ❏ Observation ❏ Opportunity for improvement ❏ Evidence of continual improvement

Finding

Objective evidence

Auditor signature	Audit coordinator signature
Management representative signature	

Internal Quality System Auditor Finding

Appendix C
Scope and Schedule of IDOT Surveillance Audit

DAY ONE

Time	Activity
8:30–9:00	Opening meeting
9:00–10:00	Conference room issues
	• Verify use of registration mark
	• Review of amendment to quality manual
	• Previous corrective action review
10:00–11:00	Progress toward measurable objectives
	Customer satisfaction and customer-specific requirements
11:00–12:30	Internal audit—QMS process
12:30–1:00	Lunch
1:00–3:00	Management review—QMS process
3:00–4:45	Corrective and preventive actions—QMS process
4:45–5:00	Day briefing

DAY TWO

Time	Activity
8:30–12:00	Material acceptance and inspection process
12:00–12:30	Lunch

| 12:30–4:45 | Construction site 1—Construction inspection and acceptance, contract changes, and construction documentation process—field activity |
| 4:45–5:00 | Day briefing |

DAY THREE

Time	Activity
8:30–12:30	Construction site 2—Construction inspection and acceptance, contract changes, and construction documentation process—field activity
12:30–1:00	Lunch
1:00–4:45	Program development—survey unit, contract changes, and construction documentation process—office activity
4:45–5:00	Day briefing

DAY FOUR

Time	Activity
8:30–11:30	Work environment and infrastructure process
11:30–1:00	CRS data collection
1:00–1:30	Lunch
1:30–3:00	Training, awareness, and competency process
3:00–4:30	Registration determination and report preparation
4:30–5:00	Closing meeting

Appendix D

Example Corrective and Preventive Action Forms

Corrective Action Request

Date			Corrective action number	
Location			Nonconformance category	

	Date due	By/assigned to	Completed initials and date
Investigation			
Implementation			
Audit			
CAR closed			

Description of issue

Investigation finding/root cause

Corrective action

Agreed to by: Date

Auditor's comments

Was the action taken effective?	If no, new corrective action number:
❏ Y ❏ N	

Preventive Action Request

	Date due	By/assigned to	Completed—initials and date
Date		Preventive action number	
Location		Preventive action category	
Investigation			
Implementation			
Audit			
PAR closed			

Description of issue

Investigation finding/root cause

Preventive action

Agreed to by: Date

Auditor's comments

Was the action taken effective?	If no, new preventive action number:
❑ Y ❑ N	

References

Bergenhenegouwen, Louise, Annemarie De Jong, Henk J. de Vries. *100 Frequently Asked Questions on the ISO 9000:2000 Series.* Milwaukee: ASQ Quality Press, 2002.

Brady, Sidney G. *Caesar's Gallic Campaigns.* New York: The Military Service Publishing Company, 1947.

Carroll, Lewis. *Alice's Adventures in Wonderland.* New York: Barnes & Noble Classics, 2004. Originally published in 1865.

Covey, Stephen R. *The 7 Habits of Highly Effective People.* New York: Fireside, 1989.

Deming, W. Edwards. *Out of the Crisis.* Cambridge, MA: Massachusetts Institute of Technology, 1982.

Ford, Henry, and Samuel Crowther. *Today and Tomorrow.* New York: Garden City, 1926.

Frank, Leonard Roy. *Quotationary.* New York: Random House, 2001.

Jones, Jeffrey M. "Trust in Government Remains Low." September 18, 2008. Available at: http://www.gallup.com/poll/110458/Trust-Government-Remains-Low.aspx. Accessed June 4, 2009.

Kaplan, Robert S., and David P. Norton. *The Strategy-Focused Organization.* Watertown, MA: Harvard Business School Press, 2001.

Langer, Ellen J. *Personal Politics: The Psychology of Making It.* Englewood Cliffs, NJ: Prentice-Hall, 1973.

Langer, Ellen J. *The Psychology of Control.* Thousand Oaks, CA: Sage Publications, 1983.

Lyons, Linda. "Social Responsibility: Will Grads Raise the Bar?" June 18, 2002. Available at: http://www.gallup.com/poll/6211/Social-Responsibility-Will-Grads-Raise-Bar.aspx. Accessed May 19, 2009.

Lombardi, Vince. "The Official Web Site of Vince Lombardi." Available at: http://www.vincelombardi.com/about/quotes4.htm. Accessed April 29, 2009.

McCullough, David. *1776.* New York: Simon & Schuster, 2005.

Rabbit, John T., and Peter A. Bergh. *The ISO 9000 Book.* White Plains, NY: Quality Resources, 1994.

Roberts, Lon. *SPC for Right-Brain Thinkers.* Milwaukee: ASQ Quality Press, 2006.

Rotherty, Brian. *ISO 9000.* Brookfield, VT: Gower, 1991.

Index